Dr. Birdley Teaches Science!

Atomic Structure and Chemical Reactions

Featuring the Comic Strip

Middle and High School

Innovative Resources for the Science Classroom

Written and Illustrated by Nevin Katz

Incentive Publications, Inc.

Nashville, Tennessee

About the Author

Nevin Katz is a teacher and curriculum developer who lives in Amherst, Massachusetts with his wife Melissa and son Jeremy.

Nevin majored in Biology at Swarthmore College and went on to earn his Master's in Education at the Harvard Graduate School of Education. He began developing curriculum as a student teacher in Roxbury, Massachusetts.

"Mr. Katz" has been teaching science over 6 years, in grades 6 through 11. He currently teaches Biology, Environmental Science, and Physical Science at Ludlow High School in Ludlow, Massachusetts.

Nevin's journey with Dr. Birdley and the cast began in the summer of 2002, when he started authoring the cartoon and using it in his science classes. From there, he developed the cartoon strip, characters, and curriculum materials. After designing and implementing the materials, he decided to develop them further and organize them into a series of books.

Cover by Geoffrey Brittingham
Edited by Jill Norris
Science Editors: K. Noel Freitas and Scott Norris

ISBN 978-0-86530-537-3

1   2   3   4   5   6   7   8   9   10   10   09   08   07

PRINTED IN THE UNITED STATES OF AMERICA
www.incentivepublications.com

TABLE OF CONTENTS

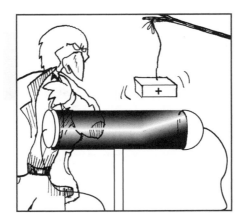

Educational Objectives

Central Goal: • To introduce cells and explain why they are the smallest units of life.
• To discuss major types of cells and differentiate between unicellular and multicellular organisms.

Chapter	Primary Objective(s)	Standards
1. Atomic Structure	To discuss the properties of the atom's subatomic particles. To explain the importance of orbitals in atomic bonding.	1, 3, 4, 8
2. Early Models of the Atom	To explain the experiments leading to early models of the atom and illustrate the characteristics of these models.	2, 12
3. Models of the Atom	To compare and contrast the Bohr and Electron cloud models.	2, 12, 8
4. Periodic Pattern	To discuss the trend in the periodic table that reflect the chemical properties of the elements.	5, 7, 11, 6
5. Atomic Bonding	To compare and contrast ionic and covalent bonding.	5, 8, 4
6. Conservation of Mass	To illustrate how mass is conserved in a chemical reaction using an experimental method and related chemical equations.	10, 9
7. Lewis Structures	To represent atoms and molecules using Lewis Structures	5, 6

National Frameworks

This page outlines the relevant state and national frameworks that the chapters relate to. After each standard, the pertinent chapters are listed.

National Science Education Standards
Science Content Standards, Grades 9-12: Chemistry

1. Matter is made of minute particles called atoms, and atoms are composed of even smaller components. These components have measurable properties, such as mass and electrical charge. (Unit 1)

2. Each atom has a positively charged nucleus surrounded by negatively charged electrons. (Units 2, 3)

3. The electric force between the nucleus and electrons holds the atom together. (Unit 1)

4. The atom's nucleus is composed of protons and neutrons, which are much more massive than electrons. (Units 1, 5)

5. Atoms interact with one another by transferring or sharing electrons that are furthest from the nucleus. These outer electrons govern the chemical properties of the element. (Units 4, 5, 7)

6. An element is composed of a single type of atom. When elements are listed in order according to the number of protons (called the atomic number), repeating patterns of physical and chemical properties identify families of elements with similar properties. (Unit 4)

7. This "Periodic Table" is a consequence of the repeating pattern of outermost electrons and their permitted energies. (Unit 4)

8. Bonds between atoms are created when electrons are paired up by being transferred or shared. (Units 1, 3, 5)

9. Substances react chemically in characteristic ways with other substances to form new substances (compounds) with different characteristic properties. (Unit 6)

10. In chemical reactions, the total mass is conserved. (Unit 6)

11. Substances often are placed in categories or groups if they react in similar ways; metals is an example of such a group. (Unit 4)

12. Scientific explanations emphasize evidence, have logically consistent arguments, and use scientific principles, models, and theories. The scientific community accepts and uses such explanations until displaced by better scientific ones. When such displacement occurs, science advances. (Unit 2, 3)

National Academies Press, 2005
http://www.nap.edu/readingroom/books/nses/

Overview of Source Cartoons

The difficulty level ranges from easy (L1) to very challenging (L3).

Cartoon	Central Concept	Challenge Level	Related Topics
Exploring the Atom	The Atom and its Electrons	L2	Ions & Electron Orbitals
The Plum Pudding Model	The Experiment that Led to Thomson's Model of the Atom	L2	Electricity and Electrons
The Gold Foil Experiment	The Experiment that Led to Rutherford's Model of the Atom	L2	The Atom's Nucleus
Defending Bohr	The Experiment that Led to Bohr's Model of the Atom	L2	Valence Electrons
Electron Cloud Model	Models of the Atom	L3	Heisenburg Uncertainty Principle
A Periodic Pattern	A Periodic Pattern	L3	The Periodic Table
Atomic Bonding	Atomic Bonding	L2	Element Groups
Ionization	How Atoms Become Ions	L2	Ions, Valence Electrons
Conservation of Mass	Conservation of Mass	L1	Acid-Base Reactions
A Chemical Equation	Conservation of Mass	L3	Naming Compounds
Balancing Act	Conservation of Mass	L3	Stoichiometry
A Structure Named Lewis	Lewis Structures	L2	Covalent Bonding

Dr. Birdley Teaches Science –
Atomic Structure and Chemical Reactions

Teacher's Guide

Contents

GREETINGS! MY NAME IS DR. BIRDLEY. I AM HERE TO EXPLAIN WHAT THIS BOOK IS ALL ABOUT.

AT FIRST GLANCE, THIS LOOKS LIKE A BOOK OF ENTERTAINING CARTOONS...

WITH HANDSOME CHARACTERS SUCH AS MYSELF.

BUT UPON FURTHER INSPECTION...

EGADS! THESE CARTOONS ARE EDUCATIONAL!

PRECISELY.

THE CHAPTERS IN THIS BOOK FOCUS FOCUS ON ATOMIC STRUCTURE AND BONDING.

EACH CARTOON COMES WITH A SET OF RELATED ASSIGNMENTS.

THEY CAN BE USED FOR LESSON TIME,

GROUP ACTIVITIES,

OR DRAMATIC READINGS.

FOLLOW ME, AND I WILL SHOW YOU HOW TO USE THEM!

KATZ '04

Dr. Birdley Teaches Science –
Atomic Structure and Chemical Reactions

The Source Cartoon

The *Source Cartoon* explains the central concepts of the overall chapter. It is usually one or two pages in length. Expect to find the following in a given source cartoon:

• A central idea with supporting details

• Visual images related to the topic being presented

• Explanations of science concepts

• A range of characters who explain the information to each other or to the reader

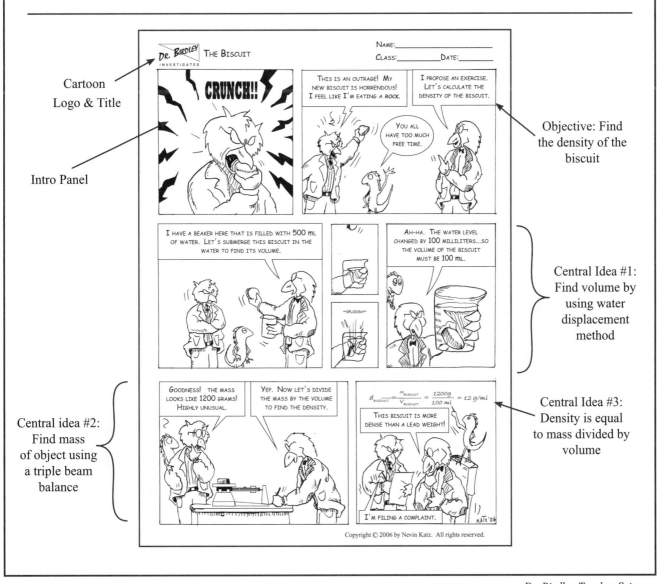

The Cartoon Profile

The *Cartoon Profile,* which outlines a source cartoon's science content, is useful for planning or teaching a lesson. Central elements include:

- The objectives in the cartoon, which are listed alongside the related state or national standards.

- The "questions for discussion" below the image, which are useful for getting students engaged and checking for understanding.

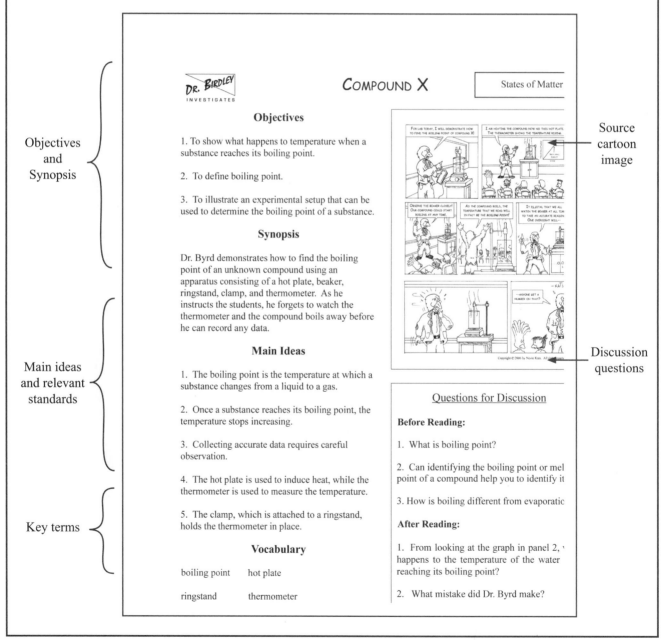

Assignments & Assessments

Supplementary assignments help students build comprehension of the central ideas in the cartoons. While quizzes assess students' knowledge of key points from a given chapter, tests check for cumulative understanding of a given section. Five of the major assignments in each chapter and one page of a sample section assessment are pictured below:

Study Questions

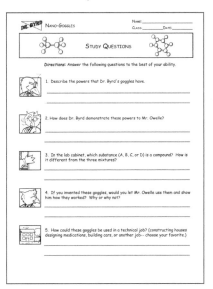

Visual Exercises

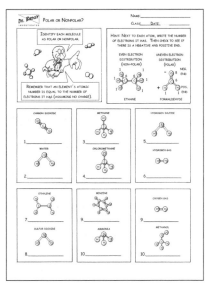

Graphic Organizer

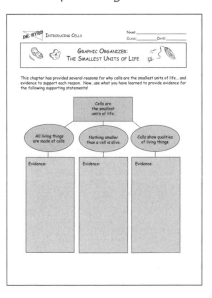

Vocabulary Build-up

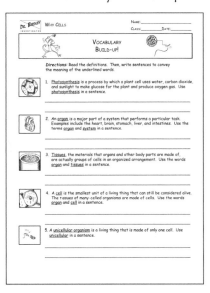

Background Article

Quiz

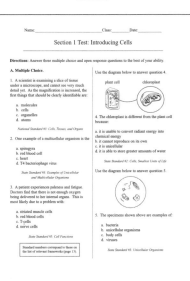

Dr. Birdley Teaches Science –
Atomic Structure and Chemical Reactions

Cell Unit: Day 1

AH! THERE YOU ARE.

YOU'RE IN LUCK! I'M ABOUT TO TEACH A LESSON INVOLVING A CARTOON AND ITS RELATED ASSIGNMENTS.

PreLesson: List four questions you have about cells.

Objectives: To discuss the importance of cells.

To introduce four levels of organization in living things.

THIS IS WHAT MY MAIN BOARD LOOKS LIKE BEFORE A LESSON.

Vocabulary:
cell
tissue
organ
system
multicellular
unicellular

AGENDA
1. PreLesson
2. Vocab Build-up
3. Read Cartoon
4. Discuss it
5. Study Questions
6. Visual Exercise
7. Lab Activity

HERE I HAVE COPIES OF THE CARTOON AND ASSIGNMENTS...

AS WELL AS THE EQUIPMENT FOR THE LAB ACTIVITY.

I CARRY THIS CLIPBOARD DURING THE LESSON.

IT CONTAINS THE CARTOON PROFILE AND COPIES OF THE HANDOUTS.

TO SEE THE RELATED EXERCISES, PROCEED TO THE NEXT PAGE!

KATZ '05

Dr. Birdley Teaches Science –
Atomic Structure and Chemical Reactions

Sample Lesson Plan

This sample lesson plan integrates materials from Unit 1 as a means of introducing cells. The overall format shown below can be applied to a range of different lessons.

Warming up the brain!

Lesson Objective: To define cells and explain their significance.

A. ***Warm-up:*** Students list what they already know and questions they have about cells.

B. ***Sharing ideas****:* The teacher reviews the warm-up with students to learn about their prior knowledge.

C. ***Vocabulary:*** Students complete the vocabulary build-up, using key words in sentences.

Reading & Discussion

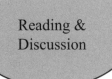

A. ***Introducing the Cartoon:*** The teacher leads a discussion on the *Before Reading* questions from the cartoon profile.

B. ***Classwide reading:*** Several student volunteers read the cartoon aloud.

C. ***Discussion:*** The teacher leads a discussion on the *After Reading* questions from the cartoon profile.

D. ***Reading in pairs:*** Students read again in pairs, highlighting key words and writing comments on a separate sheet of paper.

Practice & Application

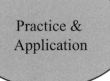

A. ***Independent Practice:*** Students complete supplementary assignments from Unit 1, which include:
- study questions
- visual exercise
- background section questions
- graphic organizer
- Unit 1 quiz

Periodically, the class reviews the answers to the exercises.

B. ***Activity:*** Students examine cell types under a microscope using different magnifications. They then draw each specimen.

CARTOONS?! BEING USED IN THE CLASSROOM? THE VERY IDEA SOUNDS PREPOSTEROUS!

RELAX, DEAN OWELLE! EACH ONE IS ALIGNED WITH SPECIFIC LEARNING OBJECTIVES.

LOOK AT THE OBJECTIVES CHART IN UNIT 1 HERE.

IT SHOWS THE PRIMARY EDUCATIONAL GOALS OF EACH CHAPTER.

HMPH.

BUT HOW CAN EDUCATORS LEARN ABOUT A CARTOON'S RELEVANCE TO THE SUBJECT MATTER?

SIMPLE! EACH CARTOON COMES WITH A CARTOON PROFILE, WHICH OUTLINES ITS SCIENCE CONTENT.

CARTOON PROFILE

LOOK! HERE WE SEE GINA SPARROW, A BIOLOGY TEACHER, PLANNING A LESSON ON THE CELL THEORY USING A CARTOON PROFILE.

AND HOW DO STUDENTS PRACTICE USING WHAT THEY LEARN FROM THEM?

THESE ASSIGNMENTS HERE REQUIRE STUDENTS TO SHOW AN UNDERSTANDING OF THE CARTOON'S CENTRAL IDEAS.

HMM. WELL, I'VE ALWAYS SAID THAT THE VISUAL NATURE OF THE CARTOON ADDS THE PERFECT KICK TO A LESSON!

KATZ '05

Dr. Birdley Teaches Science –
Atomic Structure and Chemical Reactions

THE CENTRAL PART OF ANY UNIT IS THE **SOURCE CARTOON,** WHICH EXPLAINS SCIENTIFIC IDEAS USING EXPLANATIONS AND IMAGES!

SOURCE CARTOON

But don't forget what each source cartoon comes with, Birdley.

GRAPHIC ORGANIZER

STUDY QUESTIONS

PANEL REVIEW

BACKGROUND

VISUAL EXERCISE

UNBELIEVABLE! I'M SURROUNDED BY *SUPPLEMENTARY MATERIALS!!*

CARTOON PROFILE

VOCABULARY BUILD-UP

YOU REALLY NEED TO GET A BINDER.

Dr. Birdley Teaches Science –
Atomic Structure and Chemical Reactions

ALRIGHT, CLASS...

IT'S TIME TO READ TODAY'S CARTOON!

CHRISTINE IS PASSING OUT A COPY TO EACH OF YOU. I WILL NOW NEED FOUR VOLUNTEERS TO READ THE CARTOON ALOUD TO THE CLASS!

CELIA, YOU'LL PLAY DR. BIRDLEY!

MARVIN, YOU'LL PLAY NATE!

DAN, YOU'LL PLAY MICROBE #1!

GREG, YOU'LL PLAY MICROBE #2!

YAWWN

HUH?

LIGHTS-- CAMERA--- ACTION!

As the four volunteers read the cartoon aloud, the audience listens and circles key words.

GOOD JOB! NOW ACCORDING TO THE CARTOON...

...WHY ARE CELLS IMPORTANT??

I KNOW! BECAUSE CELLS ARE THE SMALLEST UNITS OF LIFE!

KATZ'05

GOOD! LET'S KEEP REVIEWING THE CARTOON AND THEN GO TO THE STUDY QUESTIONS!

*Dr. Birdley Teaches Science –
Atomic Structure and Chemical Reactions*

Dr. Birdley! I need a group activity that gets my students hooked on science!

I'm actually preparing one as we speak! First, I cut this cartoon into panels.

I put the panels in an envelope and hand it to the students.

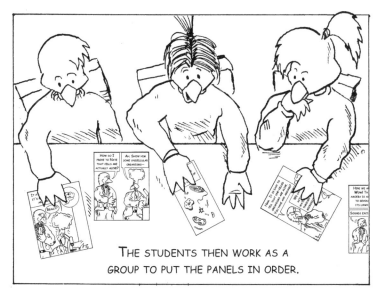

The students then work as a group to put the panels in order.

Now, using a *transparency* of the completed version...

...a student volunteer reviews the correct order and explains the cartoon's key points.

The students are hooked! They are now ready for the related exercises.

Dr. Birdley Teaches Science –
Atomic Structure and Chemical Reactions

Unit 1: Atomic Structure

Contents

SO WHY ARE ATOMS SO **IMPORTANT, YOU ASK?** WELL JUST *LOOK AROUND!* ALL THE STUFF AROUND US IS MADE UP OF ATOMS.

AND DON'T FORGET THAT ATOMS ARE THE SMALLEST OBJECTS THAT HAVE SPECIFIC IDENTITIES.

THERE ARE 110 TYPES OF ELEMENTS... AND EACH ELEMENT IS MADE OF A DISTINCT TYPE OF ATOM.

Hydrogen   Helium   Lithium

RIGHT ON.

AN ATOM'S NUCLEUS IS MADE UP OF PROTONS AND NEUTRONS. CHECK OUT THE ELECTRONS IN THE INNER AND OUTER ORBITALS.

THE ORBITALS ARE REGIONS OF SPACE AROUND THE NUCLEUS WHERE ELECTRONS MOVE.

(+) PROTON

◯ NEUTRON (1 AMU)

• ELECTRON (1/1876 AMU)

THE TINY ELECTRONS REMAIN CLOSE BECAUSE OF THE ELECTRICAL FORCES EXERTED BY THE MASSIVE NUCLEUS.

THE ORBITALS OF THE ATOM HAVE VACANCIES... KIND OF LIKE STADIUM SEATS... THAT FILL UP WITH ELECTRONS.

THE ATOM'S GOAL IS TO FILL UP ITS OUTER ORBITAL WITH ELECTRONS SO THAT IT BECOMES STABLE. THIS IS KNOWN AS A *STABLE OCTET.*

P = 10
N = 10

WHAT BETTER WAY TO DO IT THAN THROUGH **BONDING** AND CHEMICAL REACTIONS?!

Dr. Birdley Teaches Science –
Atomic Structure and Chemical Reactions

THE AMAZING ATOM

Objectives

1. To identify the atom as the smallest unit of matter with a unique identity.

2. To show the charge, mass, and location of protons, neutrons, and electrons.

3. To show how the outer electron orbital relates to atomic bonding.

Synopsis

Dr. Birdley and Jaykes discuss the atom.

Main Ideas

1. The atom is the smallest unit of matter with a unique identity.

2. Atoms are made up of positive protons, neutral neutrons, and negative electrons.

3. While protons and neutrons are in the nucleus, electrons are outside the nucleus within regions of space known as orbitals.

4. Electrons stay within their orbitals because of the electrical force exerted by the nucleus.

5. Each element is made of one type of atom.

6. An atom will react with other atoms in order to achieve a full outer orbital.

Vocabulary

orbital	stable octet	atom
proton	neutron	electron
mass	amu (atomic mass unit)	

Characters

Dr. Birdley, Jaykes

Questions for Discussion

Before Reading:

1. Why do you think atoms are important?

2. What do you think atoms are made of?

After Reading:

1. Where are protons and neutrons located?

2. Where are electrons located?

3. Why do atoms want to form bonds?

Dr. Birdley Teaches Science –
Atomic Structure and Chemical Reactions

Background: Orbitals and Bonding

Check this out. All atoms are made up of three key parts: protons, neutrons, and electrons. The protons and neutrons are in the nucleus, but electrons fly around the nucleus in regions of space known as orbitals, or shells.

Each orbital has a certain number of empty spots that can be filled with electrons. The innermost orbital can hold a maximum of two, while the second orbital out can hold a maximum of eight. The innermost orbitals get filled first. An atom is most stable when its outer orbital has all its "vacancies" filled up.

Not all atoms have a full outer orbital, so the goal of any "unstable" atom is to achieve a full outer orbital by gaining or losing electrons. Because different types of atoms have different numbers of electrons, some will want to bond more than others.

Look at the diagrams here. Lithium has only one electron in its outer orbital, so it is easiest for it to lose its outer electron so its full inner orbital becomes its outer orbital. The neon atom, on the other hand, has a full outer shell and doesn't want to bond with anything.

Lithium Atom: Unstable. 1 out of 8 electrons in its outer shell.

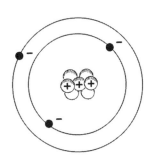

Neon Atom Stable. 8 out of 8 electrons in its outer shell.

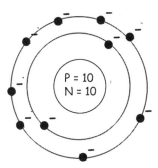

P = 10
N = 10

1. What are orbitals and why are they important?

_____

_____

2. A calcium atom has two electrons in its outer orbital. Why might it want to lose these electrons?

_____

_____

Dr. Birdley Teaches Science –
Atomic Structure and Chemical Reactions

Name:_____
Class:_____Date:_____

Study Questions

Directions: Read the related source cartoon and then answer the questions that follow.

1. Why are atoms important?

_____

_____

2. How are electrons different from protons and neutrons?

_____

_____

3. Why do electrons stay around the nucleus?

_____

_____

4. What is an orbital?

_____

_____

| 6 |
| C |
| 12.001 |

5. Why would an atom want to form bonds with other atoms?

_____

_____

Dr. Birdley Teaches Science –
Atomic Structure and Chemical Reactions

Dr. Birdley INVESTIGATES DRAWING ATOMS

NAME:_____

CLASS:_____DATE:_____

IDENTIFY AND COMPLETE EACH ATOM. MAKE SURE YOU PUT THE CORRECT NUMBER OF ELECTRONS IN EACH ORBITAL. USE YOUR PERIODIC TABLE!

No PROBLEM.

REFERENCE BOX

\# Neutrons = Atomic Mass - Atomic Number

\# Protons = Atomic Number

\# Electrons = \# Protons (for neutral atoms)

The inner orbital holds a maximum of two electrons and gets filled first.

The second orbital holds a maximum of eight electrons and gets filled after inner orbital.

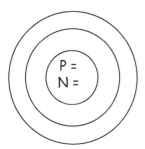

1. Atomic Number: 3

Atomic Mass: 7

Name:_____

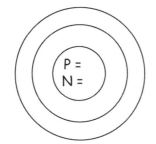

2. Atomic Number: 4

Atomic Mass: 9

Name:_____

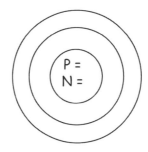

3. Atomic Number: 5

Atomic Mass: 11

Name:_____

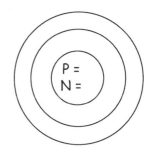

4. Atomic Number: 6

Atomic Mass: 12

Name:_____

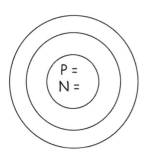

5. Atomic Number: 7

Atomic Mass: 14

Name:_____

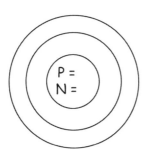

6. Atomic Number: 8

Atomic Mass: 16

Name:_____

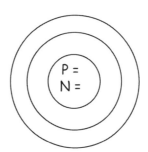

7. Atomic Number: 9

Atomic Mass: 19

Name:_____

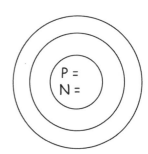

8. Atomic Number: 10

Atomic Mass: 20

Name:_____

Which two atoms could GAIN 1-2 electrons in order to complete their outer shell?

Which two atoms could LOSE 1-2 electrons in order to have a complete outer shell?

Dr. Birdley Teaches Science –
Atomic Structure and Chemical Reactions

NAME:_____

CLASS:_____ DATE:_____

PANEL REVIEW: THE STABLE OCTET

Directions: Read the panels in the space below and answer the questions that follow.

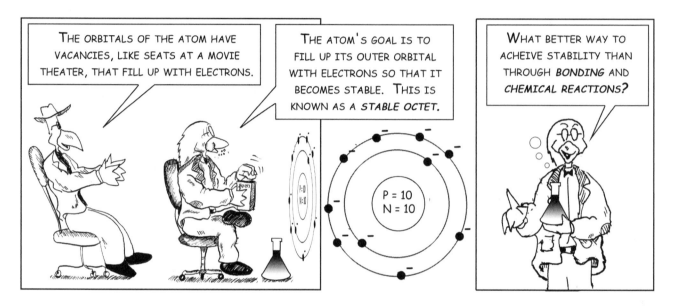

1. Identify the atom above. Why does it have a stable octet?

2. Based on the diagram, what is the maximum capacity for the inner orbital? The outer orbital?

3. Atoms can achieve a stability by gaining or losing electrons. Under each atom, list the number of electrons it would need to gain or lose in order to achieve a stable octet.

Carbon	Nitrogen	Oxygen	Fluorine	Sodium	Magnesium	Aluminum

a._____ b._____ c._____ d._____ e._____ f._____ g._____

Dr. Birdley Teaches Science –
Atomic Structure and Chemical Reactions

Vocabulary Build-up!

Directions: Use the following underlined words in sentences that convey their meaning.

1. A <u>stable octet</u> is when an atom has an outer shell that has the maximum number of electrons it can hold. Use <u>stable octet</u> in a sentence.

_____

_____

2. <u>Neutrons</u> are particles in the nucleus of an atom with no charge. Each neutron has a mass of one amu. Use <u>neutron</u> in a sentence.

_____

_____

3. <u>Electrons</u> are particles in the shells (or orbitals) of an atom that are negatively charged. Use <u>electron</u> in a sentence.

_____

_____

4. The <u>nucleus,</u> which contains protons and neutrons, is the positively charged center of the atom. Use <u>nucleus</u> in a sentence.

_____

_____

nucleus

5. <u>Orbital</u> is a region of space where electrons are most likely to be found. Use <u>electron cloud</u> in a sentence.

_____

_____

Dr. Birdley Teaches Science –
Atomic Structure and Chemical Reactions

Unit 1 Quiz: Atomic Structure

Directions: This quiz tests your knowledge of the unit's cartoon, background article, and visual exercises. Answer the following questions to the best of your ability.

1. Each element is made up of a specific type of
   (a) cell
   (b) molecule
   (c) proton
   (d) atom

2. The nucleus of an atom is made up of
   (a) electrons and neutrons
   (b) electrons and protons
   (c) neutrons and protons
   (d) protons, neutrons, and electrons

3. Valence electrons are electrons that
   (a) have a positive charge
   (b) are located at the atom's outer orbital
   (c) are especially small
   (d) are located at the lowest energy level

4. The smallest subatomic particle is the
   (a) neutron
   (b) proton
   (c) electron
   (d) isotope

5. Electrons stay close to the nucleus because of
   (a) the electrical force exerted by the nucleus
   (b) the negative charge of the neutrons
   (c) the gravitational force exerted by the electron
   (d) they are enclosed by a membrane

6. Orbitals are
   (a) connections between atoms
   (b) areas around the nucleus where electrons move
   (c) particles that atoms are made of
   (d) one or more atoms bonded together

7. Provide the following information about the subatomic particles in the table below.

	Mass	Charge	Location
Proton			
Neutron			
Electron			

Unit 2: Early Models of the Atom

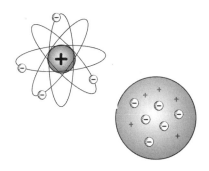

Contents

NAME:_____

CLASS:_____ DATE:_____

HEY, BIRDLEY. NEW TOY?

THIS IS A CATHODE RAY TUBE THAT JOE THOMSON BUILT IN 1897. I CAN'T GET IT TO WORK YET, THOUGH.

YOU MAY WANT TO TRY PLUGGING IT IN.

AH YES.

THERE WE ARE! A PARTICLE BEAM! PHYLL, ARE YOU READY??

YES. I AM NOW HOLDING A POSITIVELY CHARGED OBJECT ABOVE THE TUBE.

IF THE BEAM IS ATTRACTED TO SOMETHING POSITIVE, THE BEAM'S PARTICLES MUST BE NEGATIVE.

AFTER RUNNING THIS EXPERIMENT, THOMSON CONCLUDED THAT THERE WERE SMALL, NEGATIVE PARTICLES THAT CAME FROM INSIDE THE ATOM.

PARTICLE BEAM

ATOM

HE THEN DESIGNED THE *PLUM PUDDING MODEL* OF THE ATOM...

...IN WHICH THESE PARTICLES ARE LIKE "RAISINS" WITHIN A LARGER, DIFFUSE POSITIVE "PUDDING."

A DELICIOUS MODEL! BUT WHERE IS THE NUCLEUS??

EASY, PHYLL. THIS MODEL IS FROM 1897. THE NUCLEUS HADN'T BEEN DISCOVERED YET!

KATZ '07

26

Dr. Birdley Teaches Science –
Atomic Structure and Chemical Reactions

NAME:_____

CLASS:_____ DATE:_____

HERE IT IS, NORMAN. ERNEST RUTHERFORD'S **GOLD FOIL EXPERIMENT**!

DEFLECTION SCREEN

GOLD FOIL

NICE BOX.

PARTICLE EMITTER

SLIT

SO THIS GUY SHOT ALPHA PARTICLES AT GOLD FOIL TO LEARN ABOUT THE **ATOM**?

YES. HE THOUGHT THAT ATOMS HAD SUCH **LOW DENSITY** THAT THE PARTICLES WOULD SAIL RIGHT THROUGH THEM.

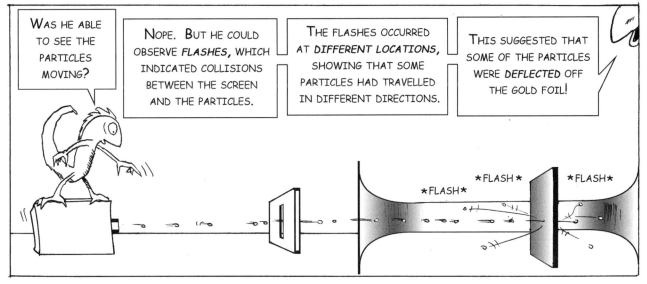

WAS HE ABLE TO SEE THE PARTICLES MOVING?

NOPE. BUT HE COULD OBSERVE **FLASHES**, WHICH INDICATED COLLISIONS BETWEEN THE SCREEN AND THE PARTICLES.

THE FLASHES OCCURRED AT **DIFFERENT LOCATIONS**, SHOWING THAT SOME PARTICLES HAD TRAVELLED IN DIFFERENT DIRECTIONS.

THIS SUGGESTED THAT SOME OF THE PARTICLES WERE **DEFLECTED** OFF THE GOLD FOIL!

FLASH *FLASH* *FLASH*

RUTHERFORD WAS ASTONISHED! HE REASONED THAT EACH ATOM MUST HAVE A **HARD CENTER** THAT SOME OF THESE PARTICLES HAD BOUNCED OFF OF.

whee!

SO WHAT HAPPENED NEXT?

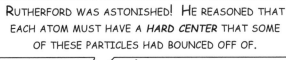

WELL, THE DISCOVERY LED HIM TO PROPOSE THE FIRST MODEL OF AN ATOM WITH A **NUCLEUS**!

THAT IS ONE SERIOUS POSITIVE CHARGE.

KATZ '07

Dr. Birdley Teaches Science –
Atomic Structure and Chemical Reactions

THE PLUM PUDDING MODEL

Objectives

1. To illustrate the experiment that led to the plum pudding model of the atom.

2. To explain the line of reasoning that led to the plum pudding model.

3. To point out the plum pudding model's key features.

Synopsis

After Gina helps Birdley turn on a cathode ray tube, Birdley explains how Joseph Thomson's experiment in 1897 led to the plum pudding model.

Main Ideas

1. In 1897, Joseph Thomson performed an experiment with a cathode ray tube, in which a beam of particles was shot through the tube.

2. The beam of particles was attracted to a positively charged object, suggesting that the particles were negative.

3. Thomson reasoned that the particles were negative and much smaller than the atom, but came from within the atom.

4. Thomson illustrated this idea with the plum pudding model, which featured small particles (the "raisins") within a positive "pudding."

5. The Plum Pudding model was the first model of the atom that had subatomic particles.

Vocabulary

plum pudding model   cathode ray tube

Characters

Dr. Birdley, Gina, Phyll

Questions for Discussion

Before Reading:

1. If an atom could be modeled using a food, what food would you use?

2. What did people know about the atom by the end of the 19th century?

3. How could people learn about something that is too small to see, even with a microscope?

After Reading:

1. What do you think the small particles were?

2. What did Thomson learn from the cathode ray tube experiment?

Dr. Birdley Teaches Science –
Atomic Structure and Chemical Reactions

THE GOLD FOIL EXPERIMENT

Objectives

1. To illustrate Ernest Rutherford's gold foil experiment, which inspired his model of the atom.

2. To explain the evidence for his experiment

3. To learn how Rutherford made sense of his results and compare his new ideas to his initial hypothesis.

4. To explain how Rutherford's conclusions led to his atomic model.

Synopsis

Birdley shows the hypothesis, procedure, results, and conclusion of the gold foil experiment. He then points out the model at the end of the comic.

Main Ideas

1. In his gold foil experiment, Ernest Rutherford used a device to shoot alpha particles at gold foil.

2. Rutherford's hypothesis was that the particles would travel straight through the atoms because he thought they had low density.

3. Rutherford found that some of the particles were deflected off the gold foil.

4. Rutherford stated that the atoms must have a positive nucleus that the atoms bounced off of. He illustrated this in his model.

Vocabulary

alpha particles   deflection screen   gold foil

Characters

Dr. Birdley, Norman

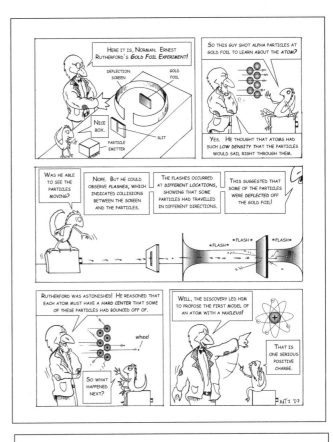

Questions for Discussion

Before Reading:

1. What did Joseph Thomson find out about the atom?

2. How was Thomson's model different from our current model of the atom?

3. What are the major parts of the scientific method?

After Reading:

1. What was Rutherford's initial hypothesis?

2. How were Rutherford's results different from his hypothesis?

3. How is Rutherford's model different from earlier models?

Dr. Birdley Teaches Science –
Atomic Structure and Chemical Reactions

 Study Questions

Directions: Read the related source cartoon and then answer the questions that follow.

 1. What happened when Dr. Birdley turned on the cathode ray tube?

_____

_____

 2. What happened as the positively charged object was brought closer to the tube? What did this reveal about the particles?

_____

_____

 3. What are two or three things Thomson concluded from his experiment?

_____

_____

 4. What are the key features of the plum pudding model?

_____

_____

 5. How was the plum pudding model different from models that came after it?

_____

_____

*Dr. Birdley Teaches Science –
Atomic Structure and Chemical Reactions*

THE GOLD FOIL EXPERIMENT

Name:_____
Class:_____Date:_____

 Study Questions

Directions: Read the related source cartoon and then answer the questions that follow.

 1. Why was Rutherford conducting the gold foil experiment?

_____

_____

 2. Describe Rutherford's experiment.

_____

_____

 3. How did Rutherford obtain evidence in his experiment?

_____

_____

 4. Did his results prove or disprove his hypothesis? Explain.

_____

_____

 5. Only one out of 2000 particles were "bounced" off of the gold foil. What does this tell you about the size of the atom's nucleus? Why?

_____

_____

Dr. Birdley Teaches Science –
Atomic Structure and Chemical Reactions

Name:_____

Class:_____Date:_____

Background: Early Models of the Atom

Directions: Use the following underlined words in sentences that convey their meaning.

Dalton's Model 2500 years ago, the Greek Philosopher Democritus had postulated that all matter was made up of tiny indivisible particles known as atoms. In 1803, John Dalton revived this theory, stating that atoms were the smallest units of matter. He went further to say that compounds contained different types of atoms in definite ratios. Dalton's model of the atom was simple and did not contain subatomic particles.

Thomson's Plum Pudding Model In 1897 the Joseph Thomson ran electricity through a cathode ray tube and saw a beam of particles. Each particle's mass was roughly 1/2000 of an atom. When he placed a positively charged object above the tube, the particles were attracted to it, leading him to believe that they were negatively charged. He thought that they originated from inside the atom. Because atoms are neutral, he reasoned that an atom would consist of negative electrons (the "raisins") surrounded by a more diffuse positive charge (the "pudding"). Hence, the plum pudding model became the first model with subatomic particles, which were to later be called electrons.

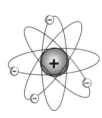

Rutherford's Model In 1911, Rutherford explored the nature of the atom by shooting alpha particles at a piece of gold foil. He predicted the particles would go right through the foil since he figured that atoms were diffuse "clouds" with low density. To his surprise, a few alpha particles bounced off the foil, leading him to believe that the atoms in the gold foil had a solid, positively charged center known as a nucleus.

1. How is the Rutherford model different from the Plum Pudding model? How is it similar?

_____

_____

_____

2. How is Dalton's model simpler than Thomson's or Rutherford's models? Why is it simpler?

_____

_____

_____

Dr. Birdley Teaches Science –
Atomic Structure and Chemical Reactions

NAME:_____

CLASS:_____DATE:_____

THESE TWO EXPERIMENTS RESULTED IN NEW ATOMIC MODELS. LABEL EACH SETUP AND MODEL WITH THE CORRECT PARTS! USE THE WORD BANK.

WORD BANK

GOLD FOIL	SLIT
PLUM PUDDING MODEL	RUTHERFORD'S MODEL
DEFLECTION SCREEN	ELECTRON (2)
CATHODE RAY TUBE	POSITIVE NUCLEUS
POSITIVE OBJECT	POSITIVE CLOUD
PARTICLE BEAM	ALPHA PARTICLE EMITTER

1. _____
2. _____
3. _____

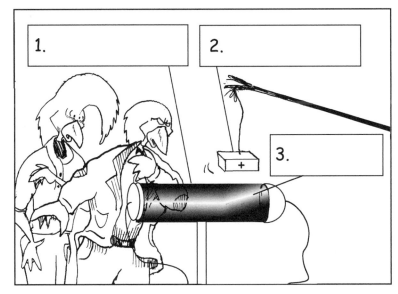

4. _____

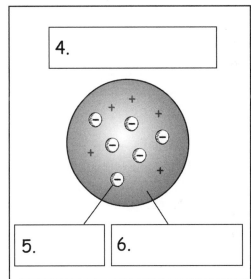

5. _____
6. _____

7. _____
8. _____
9. _____
10. _____

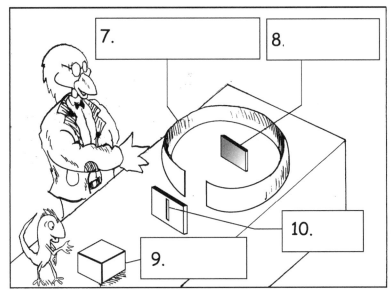

11. _____
12. _____
13. _____

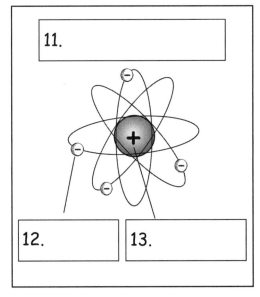

Dr. Birdley Teaches Science –
Atomic Structure and Chemical Reactions

Unit 2 Quiz: Early Models of the Atom

Directions: This quiz tests your knowledge of the chapter's cartoon, background article, and visual exercises. Answer the following questions to the best of your ability.

1. The key difference between the Rutherford model and the Plum Pudding model is that:
   - (a) only the Plum Pudding model has electrons
   - (b) only the Rutherford model has subatomic particles
   - (c) only the Plum Pudding model has a neutral charge
   - (d) only the Rutherford model has a nucleus

2. The Plum Pudding model was formulated based on experiments that utilized:
   - (a) gold foil
   - (b) a cathode ray tube
   - (c) a microscope
   - (d) an alpha particle emitter

3. The cathode ray tube revealed that:
   - (a) atoms have a nucleus
   - (b) travel in circular paths
   - (c) small, negative particles exist within the atom
   - (d) atoms can line up to form a particle beam

4. Which of the following ideas is supported by evidence from Rutherford's gold foil experiment?
   - (a) atoms are made up of alpha particles
   - (b) atoms have a small nucleus
   - (c) atoms have an electron cloud
   - (d) protons enable atoms to bond

Label each model as the a) Plum Pudding model, b) Dalton's model, or c) Rutherford's model.

5. _____

6. _____

7. _____

Label each box of the diagram with the corresponding letter of the correct part.

A. gold foil
B. particle emitter
C. slit
D. deflection screen

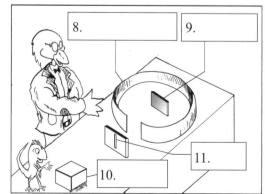

Dr. Birdley Teaches Science –
Atomic Structure and Chemical Reactions

Unit 3: The Bohr & Electron Cloud Models

Contents

NAME:_____

CLASS:_____ DATE:_____

WHAT IS THE MEANING OF THIS?! YOU'RE TEACHING YOUR STUDENTS THE **BOHR** MODEL OF THE ATOM?

YEP.

Na

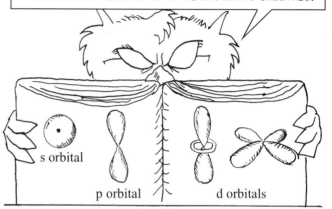

FOR GOODNESS SAKES-- GIVE THEM SCHRODINGER'S ELECTRON CLOUD MODEL! AN ELECTRON'S RANGE OF MOTION IS NOT DEFINED BY A CIRCULAR PATH-- IT IS DEFINED BY REGIONS OF SPACE KNOWN AS **ORBITALS**!

s orbital

p orbital

d orbitals

YOU AND I BOTH KNOW THAT ELECTRONS DO *NOT* ORBIT THE NUCLEUS LIKE PLANETS! WHY DO YOU INSIST ON CONFUSING YOUNG MINDS?!

Na

WELL, SORRY TO OFFEND YOU. BUT THE BOHR MODEL MAKES IT EASIER TO SEE THE MULTIPLE ORBITALS AND COUNT THE NUMBER OF ELECTRONS IN EACH ONE.

IT'S ALSO USEFUL FOR SHOWING THAT ATOMS BOND USING ELECTRONS IN THEIR OUTERMOST ORBITALS.

Na

LiF

THE MODEL MAY NOT BE TOTALLY ACCURATE, BUT NEITHER IS THIS MODEL OF THE EARTH. THE OCEAN HERE IS SOLID...NOT LIQUID!

ALL MODELS BREAK DOWN AT SOME POINT.

WHATEVER! TEACH YOUR SILLY BOHR MODEL.

OPEN-MINDEDNESS DOES NOT SEEM TO BE HIS SPECIALTY.

KATZ 06

Dr. Birdley Teaches Science –
Atomic Structure and Chemical Reactions

DR. BIRDLEY
INVESTIGATES

Panel 1:

WHAT ARE THOSE BALLOONS FOR?

I AM USING THEM FOR A LESSON ON ATOMIC STRUCTURE! THE BALLOONS REPRESENT THE ORBITALS OF ELECTRONS.

WHAT ARE ORBITALS?

Panel 2:

IN THE ELECTRON CLOUD MODEL, **ORBITALS** ARE REGIONS OF 3-DIMENSIONAL SPACE AROUND THE ATOM'S NUCLEUS WHERE THE ELECTRONS ARE MOST LIKELY TO BE.

Panel 3:

ERWIN SCHRODINGER CAME UP WITH THE MODEL IN 1926. THE IDEA IS THAT THE ELECTRON'S EXACT LOCATION IS NEVER CERTAIN...

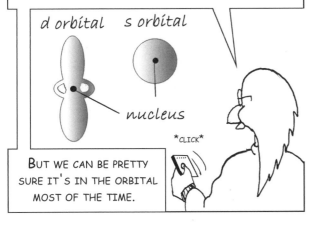

d orbital   s orbital

nucleus

CLICK

BUT WE CAN BE PRETTY SURE IT'S IN THE ORBITAL MOST OF THE TIME.

Panel 4:

WHAT ABOUT THE BOHR MODEL WHERE ELECTRONS ORBIT THE NUCLEUS LIKE PLANETS?

TECHNICALLY IT'S **WRONG**. EVEN BOHR THOUGHT SO. ELECTRON MOTION IS MORE COMPLEX THAN THAT.

Panel 5:

FORTUNATELY, THE MOVEMENT OF AN ELECTRON CAN BE DESCRIBED MATHEMATICALLY USING OUR KNOWLEDGE OF **QUANTUM MECHANICS!**

$$\mathbf{P}_R = \int_R |\psi(x,y,z)|^2 \, dV$$

Panel 6:

THEY ALWAYS DUCK OUT WHEN THEY SEE THE MATH.

$$\mathbf{P}_R = \int_R |\psi(x,y,z)|^2 \, dV$$

KATZ '06

Dr. Birdley Teaches Science –
Atomic Structure and Chemical Reactions

DEFENDING BOHR

Objectives

1) To compare and contrast the Bohr model with the electron cloud model.

2) To illustrate the concept of electron orbitals.

3) To establish the usefulness of models in science.

Synopsis

Mr. Owelle happens to see Birdley drawing Bohr models of atoms for his lesson. He criticizes the use of the Bohr model, claiming it is outdated and inaccurate. Birdley defends his use of the Bohr model by pointing out its strengths.

Main Ideas

1. The electron cloud model is more scientifically accurate than the Bohr model.

2. In the electron cloud model, orbitals are regions of 3-dimensional space where electrons are most likely to be found.

3. In the Bohr model, orbitals look more like spherical paths, similar to the orbits of planets around the sun. This model of electron motion is fundamentally wrong.

4. Despite its inaccuracies, the Bohr model is useful for clearly depicting multiple orbitals, illustrating the number of electrons in orbitals, and showing the role of valence electrons in atomic bonding.

Vocabulary

orbitals   Bohr model   electron cloud model

Characters

Dr. Birdley, Mr. Owelle, Norman

Questions for Discussion

Before Reading:

1. What is a model?

2. Why are models useful in science? Give an example!

3. Is it okay for a model to be partially inaccurate or incorrect? Explain.

After Reading:

1. Why does Owelle favor the electron cloud model?

2. Why does Mr. Birdley find the Bohr model useful?

3. What are the key differences between the two models?

Dr. Birdley Teaches Science –
Atomic Structure and Chemical Reactions

Objectives

1. To illustrate and define the concept of electron orbitals in the context of the electron cloud model.

2. To convey the complexity of electron motion.

3. To point out the main problem with the Bohr model.

Synopsis

While preparing balloon models of electron orbital, Mr. Bird explains to Celia the electron cloud model. Once he starts explaining electron motion, Celia escapes.

Main Ideas

1. Erwin Schrodinger devised the electron cloud model in 1926.

2. Electron orbitals occur in multiple shapes.

3. Electron orbitals are regions of the dimensional space where electrons are most likely to be found.

4. An electron's motion is so complex it can really be described using quantum mechanics an abstract branch of physics that deals with the motion of waves and particles.

5. Atoms may have orbitals of different shapes.

Vocabulary

orbitals   Bohr model   electron cloud model

Characters

Dr. Birdley, Mr. Owelle, Norman

Questions for Discussion

Before Reading:

1. What are the places where you are most likely to be found during a school day?

2. Draw an atom and label the protons, neutrons, and electrons.

3. Is it okay for a model to be partially inaccurate or incorrect? Explain.

After Reading:

1. Why did Celia leave?

2. What is an orbital? Why is it important?

3. What aspect(s) of the electron cloud model do the balloons help to capture?

Name:_____
Class:_____Date:_____

Study Questions

Directions: Read the related source cartoon and then answer the questions that follow.

1. Why does Owelle disapprove of the Bohr model?

_____

_____

2. What do you think the pictures in Owelle's book represent?

_____

_____

3. How are the orbitals in the electron cloud model different from the electron paths illustrated in the Bohr model?

_____

_____

4. How is the Bohr model useful as a teaching tool? Try to give two reasons.

_____

_____

5. What is Dr. Birdley's point about models? How does this relate to the Bohr model?

_____

_____

Dr. Birdley Teaches Science –
Atomic Structure and Chemical Reactions

Name:_____
Class:_____Date:_____

Study Questions

Directions: Read the related source cartoon and then answer the questions that follow.

1. What do Dr. Birdley's balloons represent?

_____

_____

2. What are orbitals in this case?

_____

_____

3. Who came up with the electron cloud model and when? Describe one or more of his central ideas.

_____

_____

4. How is the Bohr model different from the electron cloud model? Why is the Bohr model incorrect?

_____

_____

$$P_R = \int_R |\psi|$$

5. What branch of physics can be used to describe the motion of an electron? How does Celia respond to learning this?

_____

_____

Dr. Birdley Teaches Science –
Atomic Structure and Chemical Reactions

Background: Bohr vs. Electron Cloud Model

Directions: Read the following passages and answer the questions that follow.

The Bohr Model. In 1913, Neils Bohr came up with an idea of how electrons moved around the nucleus. He thought that the electrons occupied different circular orbits, or energy levels, and revolved around the nucleus in a circular pattern. Each orbital had a certain capacity for electrons. (Ex. the first orbital had a maximum of two electrons, the second orbital could hold eight electrons, etc.) The outer orbitals were the higher energy levels.

Soon after designing the model, Bohr realized that if the electrons moved like planets, they would ultimately be pulled into the nucleus because they would lose the energy needed to maintain their orbit. Because of this discrepancy he discarded his model. However, we still use it today to clearly illustrate numbers of electrons and different energy levels.

Schrodinger's Electron Cloud Model. In 1926, Erwin Schrodinger stated that electrons did not move in circular paths. Instead, he described their motion with a series of mathematical equations. The basic idea is that the motion of electrons is so fast, their location can only be measured in terms of probability. In this case, the orbitals are not circular paths, but regions of space where electrons are most likely to be found. Some of them also have non-circular shapes, as shown in the related source cartoons.

1. How is the electron (cloud) model different from the Bohr Model?

_____

_____

_____

2. Explain two strengths and two weaknesses of the Bohr model.

_____

_____

_____

_____

NAME:_____

CLASS:_____DATE:_____

DESCRIBE THE KEY FEATURES OF EACH
ATOMIC MODEL. USE THE WORD BANK.

KATZ '06

WORD BANK

NUCLEUS	POSITIVE	CIRCULAR
PROTONS	NEGATIVE	PATHS
NEUTRONS	CHARGE	DIFFUSE
ELECTRONS	PROBABILITY	ORBITALS
	SPACE	

PLUM PUDDING MODEL

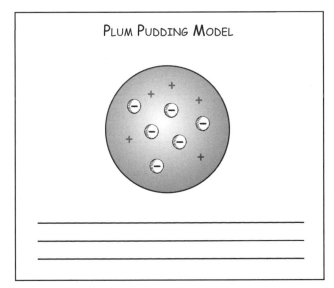

_____
_____
_____

RUTHERFORD'S MODEL

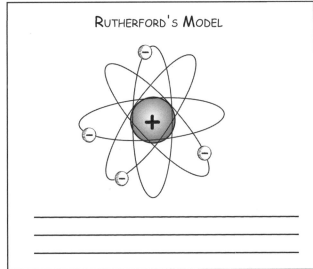

_____
_____
_____

BOHR MODEL

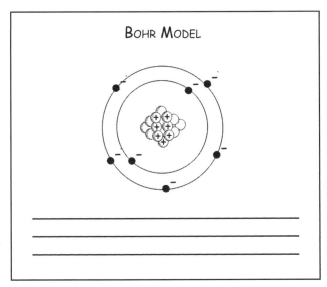

_____
_____
_____

ELECTRON CLOUD MODEL

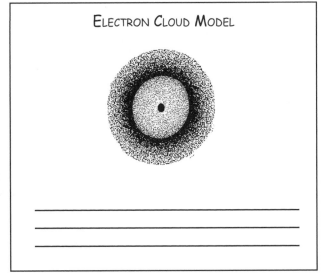

_____
_____
_____

Dr. Birdley Teaches Science –
Atomic Structure and Chemical Reactions

Name:_____ Class:_____ Date:_____

Unit 3 Quiz: Atomic Models

Directions: For each scientist, give a description of the model, and one or two new ideas that the model illustrates.

Scientist	Description of Model	New ideas the model introduced
1. J. J. Thomson's Plum Pudding Model		
2. Ernest Rutherford's Model		
3. Neils Bohr's Model		
4. Erwin Schrodinger's Electron Cloud Model		

5. If the Bohr model is no longer accurate, why is it still taught today?_____

_____

_____

Label each model as the a) Rutherford Model, b) Electron Cloud Model, or c) Bohr Model.

6. _____   7. _____   8. _____

                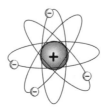

Dr. Birdley Teaches Science –
Atomic Structure and Chemical Reactions

Unit 4: Periodicity

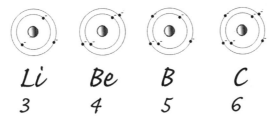

Li Be B C
3   4   5 6

Contents

TODAY, CHRISTINA WILL GIVE YOU A LESSON ON VALENCE ELECTRONS AND THE PERIODIC TABLE.

GOOD MORNING!

SO WHAT ARE VALENCE ELECTRONS? THEY ARE ELECTRONS IN AN ATOM'S OUTER SHELL THAT FORM BONDS WITH ELECTRONS FROM OTHER ATOMS.

valence electrons

Beryllium Atom (Be)

LET'S LOOK AT THE ATOMS FROM TWO PERIODS OF THE PERIODIC TABLE AND EXAMINE THEIR VALENCE ELECTRONS.

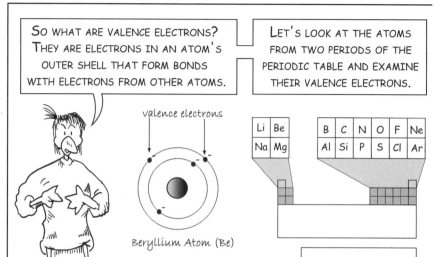

Li	Be		B	C	N	O	F	Ne
Na	Mg		Al	Si	P	S	Cl	Ar

NOW LOOK! IN EACH PERIOD, WE SEE THAT THE NUMBER OF VALENCE ELECTRONS IN AN ATOM INCREASES FROM *LEFT* TO *RIGHT*!

BECAUSE THE NUMBER OF VALENCE ELECTRONS DETERMINES HOW THE ELEMENT REACTS WITH OTHER SUBSTANCES...

...WE CAN PREDICT AN ELEMENT'S *CHEMICAL PROPERTIES* BASED ON ITS POSITION IN THE PERIODIC TABLE.

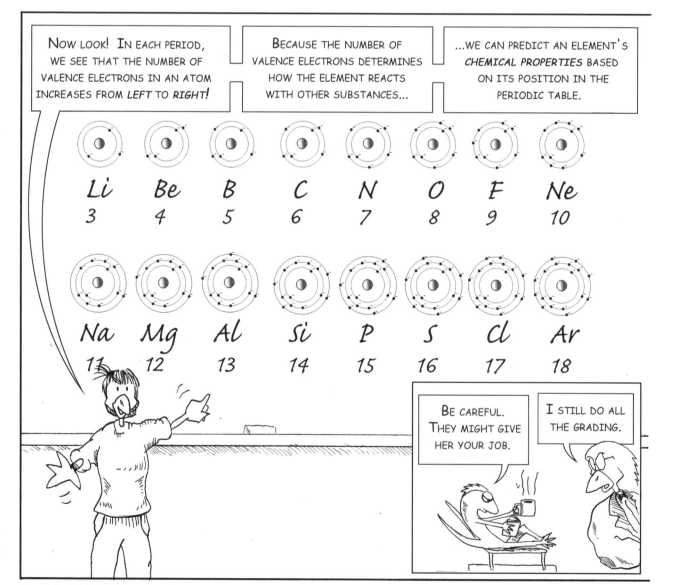

Li	Be	B	C	N	O	F	Ne
3	4	5	6	7	8	9	10

Na	Mg	Al	Si	P	S	Cl	Ar
11	12	13	14	15	16	17	18

BE CAREFUL. THEY MIGHT GIVE HER YOUR JOB.

I STILL DO ALL THE GRADING.

Dr. Birdley Teaches Science –
Atomic Structure and Chemical Reactions

A PERIODIC PATTERN

Objectives

1. To define valence electrons and emphasize their importance in bonding.

2. To relate the number of valence electrons to an element's reactivity and chemical properties.

3. To show how the pattern in the periodic table allows us to predict an element's chemical properties.

Synopsis

Celia gives a lesson on a pattern in the periodic table.

Main Ideas

1. The number of valence electrons an atom determines how the atom bonds with other atoms.

2. An atom's bonding tendencies determine how the element reacts with other substances.

3. In each period of the periodic table, the number of valence electrons increase from left to right.

4. Because the number of valence electrons determines reactivity, we can predict the chemical properties of an element based on its position in the periodic table.

Vocabulary

valence electrons   chemical properties

periodicity   reactivity

Characters

Dr. Birdley, Celia, Students

Questions for Discussion

Before Reading:

1. How many rows are in the periodic table?

2. How are the elements arranged?

3. What does the atomic number indicate about an element?:

4. Why are electrons essential in atoms?

After Reading:

1. Why are valence electrons important?

2. What is the pattern in the periodic table?

3. Why is this pattern important?

Periodic Table

Dr. Birdley Teaches Science –
Atomic Structure and Chemical Reactions

NAME:_____

CLASS:_____ DATE:_____

Background:
A Periodic Pattern

In the cartoon, Christina shows Bohr models for two periods in the periodic table. The pattern in each period is the same: the number of valence electrons increases from left to right. This is important because the number of electrons determines bonding. Look at the diagram below and read how their bonding demonstrates some the bonding properties in elements.

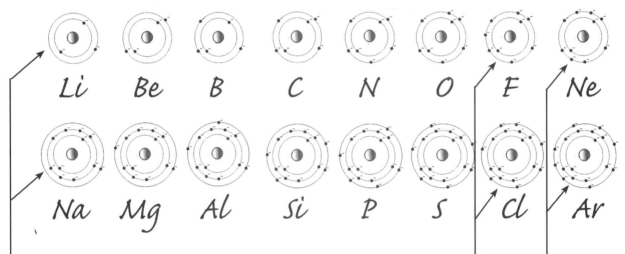

Both Lithium (Li) and Sodium (Na) have only one valence electron and BADLY want to give it up so they can have a full outer shell. As a result, they will bond with elements that want to take electrons...like Chlorine (Cl).

Chlorine (Cl) and Fluorine (F) have seven valence electrons. Atoms become much more stable when they lose or gain an electron to create a full valence shell so they will bond with elements that tend to give up valence electrons...like Sodium or Magnesium.

Because Argon and Neon have full outer shells, they do not want to bond with any elements. As you can see, each one has eight valence electrons.

1. How are Lithium and Sodium similar?_____

_____

_____

2. Why would a Sodium atom readily bond with Chlorine atom?_____

_____

_____

Dr. Birdley Teaches Science –
Atomic Structure and Chemical Reactions

Name:_____
Class:_____Date:_____

 Study Questions

Beryllium Atom (Be)

Directions: Read the related source cartoon and then answer the questions that follow.

1. Where are valence electrons located?

_____

_____

2. How do valence electrons relate to the formation of molecules?

_____

_____

3. What is the pattern that Christina points out in the periodic table?

_____

_____

4. What does the number of valence electrons tell you about a given element?

_____

_____

5. How is it possible to predict the properties of an element based on its position in the periodic table?

_____

_____

Dr. Birdley Teaches Science –
Atomic Structure and Chemical Reactions

- Describe the pattern below in detail.
- Use the words in the word bank.
- Use specific atoms as examples.
- Explain the importance of the pattern.

| Li | Be | | | B | C | N | O | F | Ne |
| Na | Mg | | | Al | Si | P | S | Cl | Ar |

KATZ '04

WORD BANK

VALENCE	RIGHT
ELECTRONS	TABLE
BONDING	PERIODIC
REACTIVITY	PERIODS
INCREASES	GROUP
LEFT	ATOM'S
SAME	NUMBER

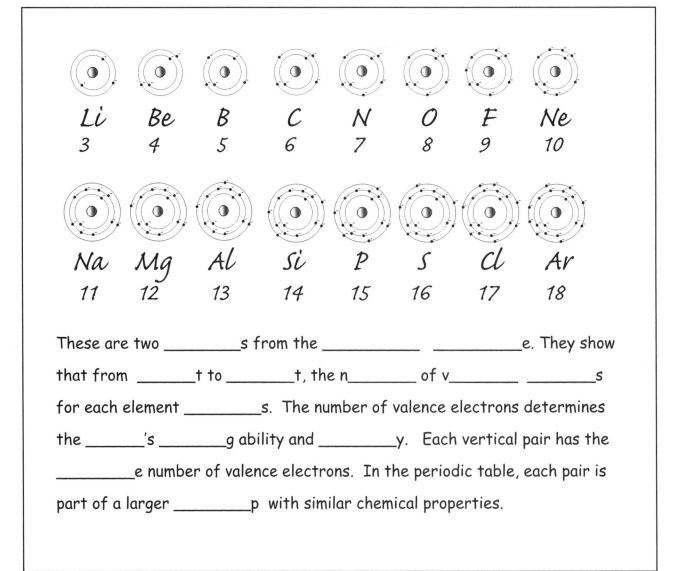

Li	Be	B	C	N	O	F	Ne
3	4	5	6	7	8	9	10

Na	Mg	Al	Si	P	S	Cl	Ar
11	12	13	14	15	16	17	18

These are two _____s from the _____ _____e. They show

that from _____t to _____t, the n_____ of v_____ _____s

for each element _____s. The number of valence electrons determines

the _____'s _____g ability and _____y.   Each vertical pair has the

_____e number of valence electrons. In the periodic table, each pair is

part of a larger _____p with similar chemical properties.

Dr. Birdley Teaches Science –
Atomic Structure and Chemical Reactions

Vocabulary Build-up!

Directions: Use the following underlined words in sentences that convey their meaning.

1. A <u>period</u> is one row in the periodic table. Use <u>period</u> in a sentence.

_____

_____

2. <u>Valence electrons</u> are electrons in the outer shell of the atom that participate in bonding.

_____

_____

3. Atoms <u>bond</u> when they connect by sharing or transferring electrons. Use <u>bond</u> in a sentence.

_____

_____

4. <u>Physical properties</u> are qualities of a substance that can be observed without changing what the object is made of. Use <u>physical properties</u> in a sentence.

_____

_____

5. <u>Chemical properties</u> are qualities of a substance that can only be observed by changing its composition. Use <u>chemical properties</u> in a sentence.

_____

_____

Dr. Birdley Teaches Science –
Atomic Structure and Chemical Reactions

Unit 4 Quiz: A Periodic Pattern

Directions: This quiz tests your knowledge of the unit's cartoon, background article, and visual exercises. Answer the following questions to the best of your ability.

1. The number of valence electrons increases
   - (a) from left to right across a period.
   - (b) from right to left across a period.
   - (c) from top to bottom of a group.
   - (d) from bottom to top of a group.

2. The bonding ability of an element is determined by
   - (a) the number of neutrons.
   - (b) the charge of the neutrons.
   - (c) the number of valence electrons.
   - (d) the number electrons at the inner shell.

3. Which of the following provides the least amount of information on an element's chemical properties?
   - (a) position on the periodic table
   - (b) number of valence electrons
   - (c) the vertical group that an element belongs to
   - (d) the horizontal period that an element belongs to

4. Which of the following elements have a full outer shell of electrons?
   - (a) elements on the far right of the periodic table
   - (b) elements on the far left on the periodic table
   - (c) elements at the top of the periodic table
   - (d) elements at the bottom of the periodic table

Directions: Explain what the diagram illustrates. Then, explain how it can tell you about an element's chemical properties.

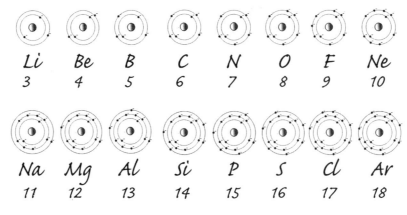

Li	Be	B	C	N	O	F	Ne
3	4	5	6	7	8	9	10

Na	Mg	Al	Si	P	S	Cl	Ar
11	12	13	14	15	16	17	18

_____

_____

_____

Dr. Birdley Teaches Science – Atomic Structure and Chemical Reactions

Unit 5: Atomic Bonding

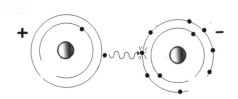

Contents

NAME:_____

CLASS:_____ DATE:_____

THE ATOM. A CONCENTRATED CLUSTER OF PROTONS AND NEUTRONS, SURROUNDED BY SWARMING ELECTRONS THAT MOVE AT TREMENDOUS SPEEDS.

COMPARED TO PROTONS AND NEUTRONS, ELECTRONS ARE A GREAT DEAL SMALLER....

...BUT DESPITE THEIR SMALL SIZE, THEY ARE EXTREMELY CRITICAL TO SHAPING THE WORLD AS WE KNOW IT.

PUT SIMPLY, ELECTRONS ALLOW ATOMS TO CONNECT WITH EACH OTHER BY FORMING *BONDS*.

IN AN IONIC BOND, AN ATOM GIVES AN ELECTRON TO ANOTHER ATOM, RESULTING IN EACH ATOM BEING CHARGED.

IN A COVALENT BOND, THE ATOMS SHARE ELECTRONS IN ORDER TO ACHIEVE STABLE OUTER ELECTRON SHELLS.

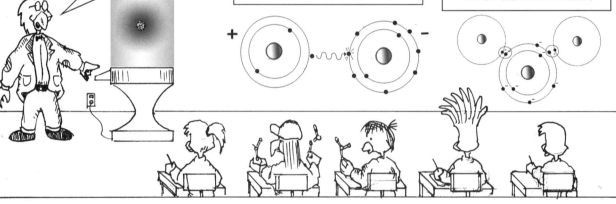

ATOMS BOND TO FORM THE MOLECULES THAT EVERYTHING AROUND US IS COMPOSED OF.

SO YOU'RE SAYING THAT THIS BENZENE MOLECULE IS BASICALLY A BUNCH OF ATOMS HOLDING HANDS AND SINGING KUMBAYAH?

NOT REALLY. IT'S A BUNCH OF ATOMS FORMING COVALENT BONDS AND SINGING KUMBAYAH.

HE ALWAYS TAKES THE FUN OUT OF MY ANALOGIES.

Dr. Birdley Teaches Science –
Atomic Structure and Chemical Reactions

NAME:_____

CLASS:_____DATE:_____

HEY. AREN'T YOU A NEUTRAL LITHIUM ATOM? DON'T SEE TOO MANY OF YOU AROUND. WHAT'S IT LIKE BEING THE SMALLEST UNIT OF MATTER?

10^{-10} m

NOT THAT IT'S ANY OF MY BUSINESS, BUT THAT CHLORINE ATOM JUST SWIPED YOUR ELECTRON.

GUESS I SHOULD CALL YOU "ION." SO HOW DO YOU LIKE THAT FULL OUTER SHELL?

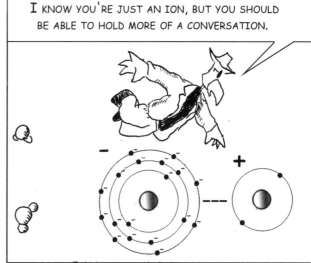

I KNOW YOU'RE JUST AN ION, BUT YOU SHOULD BE ABLE TO HOLD MORE OF A CONVERSATION.

WELL, BETTER BE ON MY WAY. CONGRATULATIONS ON ACHIEVING STABILITY.

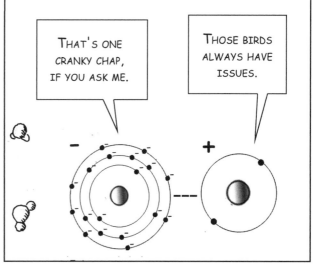

THAT'S ONE CRANKY CHAP, IF YOU ASK ME.

THOSE BIRDS ALWAYS HAVE ISSUES.

Dr. Birdley Teaches Science –
Atomic Structure and Chemical Reactions

Objectives

1. To introduce two major types of bonding: ionic and covalent.

2. To establish the role of electrons as particles that enable atoms to bond.

3. To point out that bonding is necessary for the formation of molecules.

Synopsis

Dr. Birdley give a lesson on bonding.

Main Ideas

1. Electrons are a great deal smaller than the atom's nucleus.

2. Electrons enable atoms to form bonds.

3. Ionic bonds involve one atom donating electrons to another atom.

4. Atoms that donate an electron in an ionic bond take on a positive charge.

5. Atoms that accept an electron in an ionic bond take on a negative charge.

6. Covalent bonds involve two atoms sharing electrons.

7. Bonding results in the formation of molecules.

Vocabulary

ions   ionic bonds   covalent bonds

Characters

Dr. Birdley, Greg, other students

Questions for Discussion

Before Reading:

1. How do molecules form?

2. What makes electrons different from protons and neutrons?

3. What are bonds and why are they important?

After Reading:

1. How do electrons relate to bonding?

2. What would the universe be like if electrons did not exist?

3. Describe the central qualities of ionic and covalent bonds.

Dr. Birdley Teaches Science –
Atomic Structure and Chemical Reactions

Objectives

1. To illustrate how atoms become ions.

2. To explain why atoms become ions.

3. To relate ionization to full valence shells and charge.

Synopsis

Jaykes, who has been miniaturized to the size of the atom, tries to strike up a conversation with a lithium atom that ionically bonds to a chlorine atom.

Main Ideas

1. The lithium atom donates an electron to the chlorine atom.

2. When the lithium atom loses the electron, it is called an ion.

3. The lithium atom develops +1 charge because it has more three positive protons and two negative electrons.

4. The chlorine atom develops –1 charge because it has 18 electrons and 17 protons.

5. After losing its electron, the lithium ion has a full outer shell and has achieved stability. The same is the case for the sodium ion.

6 The process of losing or gaining an electron and developing a charge is called ionization.

Vocabulary

ionization   ion   outer shell

Characters

Jaykes and two atoms

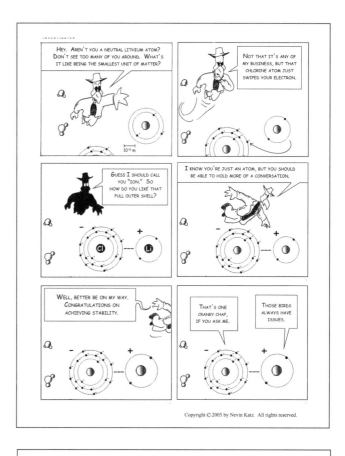

Questions for Discussion

Before Reading:

1. Why do atoms like to bond?

2. What does it mean when an atom has a charge?

3. Why do atoms develop charges?

After Reading:

1. How is the lithium ion different from the neutral lithium atom?

2. What compound forms during the comic? (Lithium Chloride, LiCl)

3. Why does the chlorine atom become negative?

Dr. Birdley Teaches Science –
Atomic Structure and Chemical Reactions

Name:_____

Class:_____Date:_____

Study Questions

Directions: Read the related source cartoon and then answer the questions that follow.

 1. Why are electrons so important?

_____

_____

 2. How are covalent bonds different from ionic bonds?

_____

_____

 3. Which element is the negatively charged ion? Why does accepting an electron cause this atom to take on a partially negative charge?

_____

_____

 4. Which element is the positively charged ion? Why does donating the electron cause this atom to take on a partially positive charge?

_____

_____

 5. How does bonding relate to the formation of molecules?

_____

_____

Dr. Birdley Teaches Science –
Atomic Structure and Chemical Reactions

 IONIZATION

Name:_____
Class:_____Date:_____

Study Questions

Directions: Read the related source cartoon and then answer the questions that follow.

 1. How does the lithium atom become an ion?

_____

_____

 2. Why did the lithium atom want to lose an electron?

_____

_____

 3. Why does the lithium atom develop a positive charge?

_____

_____

 4. Which is more stable: neutral chlorine atoms or chlorine ions? Why?

_____

_____

 5. Which do you think are fewer in number: neutral unbonded lithium atoms or lithium ions that have connected with other atoms? Why?

_____

_____

Dr. Birdley Teaches Science –
Atomic Structure and Chemical Reactions

BACKGROUND: IONIC AND COVALENT BONDING

An atom will form bonds to achieve a full outer shell of electrons. This may involve sharing, donating, or accepting electrons. To learn more about how this works, read about two types of bonds below:

COVALENT BONDS

Covalent bonds involve two atoms sharing electrons. They usually occur between two non-metals. When carbon, oxygen, and hydrogen bond together, many of their bonds are covalent. The water molecule pictured below is held together by covalent bonds.

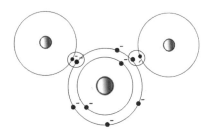

Because each atom still has equal numbers of protons and electrons, atoms that are covalently bonded do not have significant charges. Notice that the atoms are using electrons in their outer shell to bond.

IONIC BONDS

Ionic bonds involve one atom giving one or more electrons to a receiving atom. An atom becomes an ion when it has unequal numbers of protons and electrons. There are two types: anions and cations. Look at the picture below that depicts Lithium bonding to Fluorine:

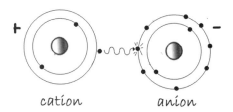

cation   anion

Because the "donor" atom loses an electron, it develops a positive charge and becomes a cation. Because the "accepter" atom gains an electron, it develops a negative charge and becomes an anion.

---

1. What is the difference between an ionic and covalent bond?

---

2. Why does lithium take on a positive charge when it bonds to Fluorine? Why does Fluorine take on a negative charge?

Vocabulary & Practice Problems

Directions: Use the following underlined words in sentences that convey their meaning.

1. An <u>ion</u> is a charged atom. Ions have unequal numbers of protons and electrons. Use the word <u>ion</u> in a sentence.

_____

_____

2. An <u>ionic bond</u> occurs when an element (usually a metal) donates electron(s) to non-metal element. Use <u>ionic bond</u> in a sentence.

_____

_____

3. A <u>covalent bond</u> involves the sharing of electrons between two non-metal elements. Use the term <u>covalent</u> in a sentence.

_____

_____

4. Identify each molecule as ionic (I) or covalent (C).

a. ___H_2O b. ___LiF   c. ___$CaCl_2$ d. ___CH_4

e. ___$MgCl_2$ f. ___NaCl   g. ___H_2SO_4 h. ___$AlCl_3$

5. The charge of an atom is equal to the number of electrons it gains or loses.

If calcium loses two electrons, what is its charge? _____

If chlorine gains one electron, what is its charge? _____

Dr. Birdley Teaches Science –
Atomic Structure and Chemical Reactions

NAME:_____
CLASS:_____DATE:_____

MINI-COMIC: IONIC FORMULAS

Directions: Read the panel in the space below. Answer the questions that follow.

1. How is an ion different from a normal atom?

2. How do you know if you've written an ionic formula correctly?

3. Write the formula when the correct number of Calcium (Ca^{+2}) ions is combined with the appropriate number of Chlorine (Cl^{-1}) ions.

4. Write the formula when the correct number of Lithium (Li^{+1}) ions is combined with the appropriate number of Oxygen (O^{-2}) ions.

Dr. Birdley Teaches Science –
Atomic Structure and Chemical Reactions

DR. BIRDLEY
INVESTIGATES

BECOMING AN ION

NAME:_____

CLASS:_____DATE:_____

WRITE THE NAME AND SYMBOL FOR EACH ELEMENT. THEN WRITE THE CHARGE IT DEVELOPS WHEN IT BECOMES AN ION.

ATOMIC NUMBERS

HYDROGEN - 1   SODIUM - 11

CHLORINE - 17   FLOURINE - 9

LITHIUM - 3   MAGNESIUM - 12

HELIUM - 2   CARBON - 6

EACH BOX ILLUSTRATES *IONIZATION:* WHEN AN ATOM GAINS OR LOSES AN ELECTRON AND BECOMES AN ION.

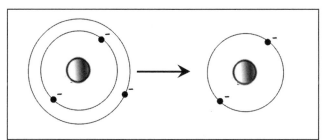

1. Name:_____Symbol:____Charge:___

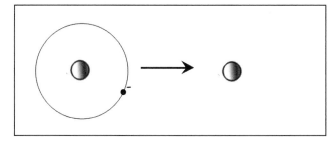

2. Name:_____Symbol:____Charge:___

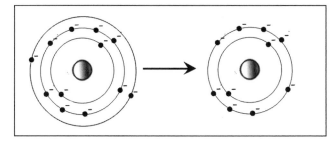

3. Name:_____Symbol:____Charge:___

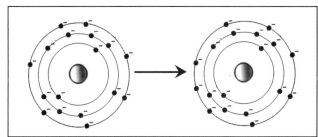

4. Name:_____Symbol:____Charge:___

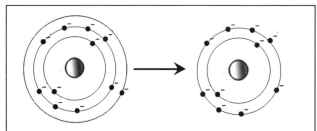

5. Name:_____Symbol:____Charge:___

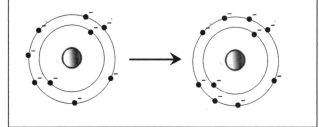

6. Name:_____Symbol:____Charge:___

Dr. Birdley Teaches Science –
Atomic Structure and Chemical Reactions

PRACTICE WITH IONIC FORMULAS

NAME:_____

CLASS:_____DATE:_____

FOR EACH PAIR OF IONS, WRITE AN IONIC FORMULA WITH A BALANCED CHARGE. THEN FIND ITS MOLECULAR MASS.

WELL LOOK HERE. ATOMIC MASSES.

Atomic Masses

Lithium - 7	Chlorine - 35
Oxygen - 16	Flourine - 19
Hydrogen - 1	Copper - 64
Calcium - 40	Magnesium - 24
Aluminum - 27	Phosphorous - 31
Iron - 56	Sulfur - 32

Li^+ and Cl^{-1}

Mg^{+2} and Cl^{-1}

Al^{+3} and F^{-1}

Fe^{+3} and O^{-2}

1. Formula:_____

Molecular Mass:_____

2. Formula:_____

Molecular Mass:_____

3. Formula:_____

Molecular Mass:_____

4. Formula:_____

Molecular Mass:_____

Ca^{+2} and F^{-1}

Cu^{+2} and SO_4^{-2}

Cu^{+1} and PO_4^{-3}

H^{+1} and O_2^{-2}

5. Formula:_____

Molecular Mass:_____

6. Formula:_____

Molecular Mass:_____

7. Formula:_____

Molecular Mass:_____

8. Formula:_____

Molecular Mass:_____

9. Which molecule has the smallest molecular mass?_____

10. Which molecule has the greatest molecular mass?_____

Dr. Birdley Teaches Science –
Atomic Structure and Chemical Reactions

NAME:_____

CLASS:_____DATE:_____

PANEL REVIEW: IONS

Directions: Review the panel in the space below and answer the questions that follow.

PUT SIMPLY, ELECTRONS ALLOW ATOMS TO CONNECT WITH EACH OTHER BY FORMING *BONDS.*

IN AN IONIC BOND, AN ATOM GIVES AN ELECTRON TO ANOTHER ATOM, RESULTING IN EACH ATOM BEING CHARGED.

IN A COVALENT BOND, THE ATOMS SHARE ELECTRONS IN ORDER TO ACHIEVE STABLE OUTER ELECTRON SHELLS.

cation   anion

1. In the space above, label the following atoms with their atomic symbols: Flourine, Lithium, Oxygen, and Hydrogen (2).

2. The atom that is the cation is _____.

3. The atom that is the anion is _____.

4. Which type of bond involves the atoms developing charges? _____.

5. Why does one atom have a positive charge?

6. Why does one atom have a negative charge?

7. Why do atoms want to bond?

Dr. Birdley Teaches Science –
Atomic Structure and Chemical Reactions

Unit 5 Quiz: Bonding

Directions: This quiz tests your knowledge of the unit's cartoon, background article, and visual exercises. Answer the following questions to the best of your ability.

1. Atoms bond covalently when they _____ electrons.

   (a) share electrons

   (b) donate electrons

   (c) develop a positive charge

   (d) develop a negative charge

2. Atoms have charges when they have

   (a) incomplete outer orbitals

   (b) lost one or more neutrons

   (c) unequal numbers of protons and electrons

   (d) eight valence electrons

3. One or more calcium ions (Ca^{+2}) combine with one or more chlorine ions (Cl^{-1}). What is the resulting formula?

   (a) Ca_2Cl_2

   (b) $CaCl_2$

   (c) Ca_2Cl

   (d) $CaCl$

4. Which of the following is the most plausible way an oxygen atom becomes an ion with a charge of -2?

   (a) it loses two electrons

   (b) it gains two electrons

   (c) it loses two protons

   (d) it gains two protons

5. Both ionic and covalent bonding are similar in that both involve:

   (a) atoms developing charges

   (b) one atom gaining an electron

   (c) two or more electrons being shared

   (d) atoms trying to complete their valence shells

6. If an atom bonds ionically, which of the following is least likely to happen?

   (a) it becomes less stable

   (b) develops a charge

   (c) it loses an electron

   (d) it gains an electron

Identify each type of bonding as ionic or covalent.

7. _____

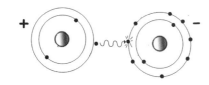

8. _____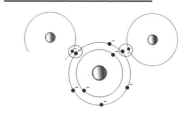

Dr. Birdley Teaches Science –
Atomic Structure and Chemical Reactions

Unit 6: Conservation of Mass

Contents

NAME:_____

CLASS:_____ DATE:_____

SO WE HAVE *ACETIC ACID* AND *BAKING SODA* SEALED IN A PLASTIC BAG HERE.

NICE! THE SCALE SHOWS THAT THEIR COMBINED MASS IS 888 g.

NOW SQUOOSH THE SUBSTANCES TOGETHER SO THAT THEY REACT.

WHOAH. THE BAG IS INFLATING!

SO WHAT DO YOU THINK THE MASS OF THE PRODUCTS WILL BE?

WELL, WHEN THE ACETIC ACID REACTS WITH BAKING SODA...

...BONDS ARE *BROKEN* AND *REMADE* BETWEEN DIFFERENT ATOMS.

THEN, THE ATOMS ARE RECOMBINED AND NEW MOLECULES FORM.

IF THE BAG IS SEALED, THIS REACTION IS HAPPENING IN A CLOSED SYSTEM, AND THE NUMBER OF ATOMS IS *CONSERVED*. SO I THINK THE MASS OF THE PRODUCTS SHOULD STAY THE SAME AND STILL BE 888 g.

AH-HA. THE PRODUCTS' MASS IS 887.9 g! WONDER WHAT HAPPENED TO THAT 0.1 GRAM.

BIRDLEY! THIS BAG EXPERIMENT WAS A DISMAL FAILURE! THE MASS OF MY PRODUCT IS 50 GRAMS LESS THAN THE MASS OF MY REACTANTS!

YOU MAY WANT TO CHECK YOUR BAG.

KATZ '06

Dr. Birdley Teaches Science –
Atomic Structure and Chemical Reactions

$$H_2O + CO_2$$

Water   Carbon Dioxide

AH! THERE YOU ARE.

YOU'RE JUST IN TIME TO REVIEW THE CHEMICAL REACTION WE TRIED OUT IN LAB TODAY.

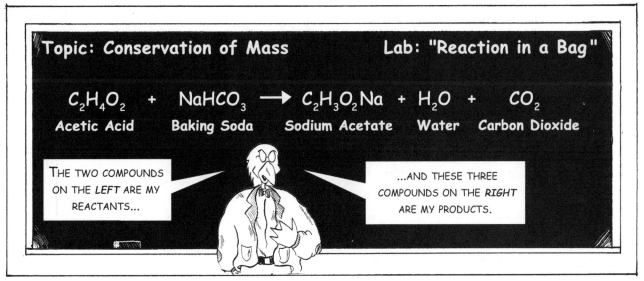

Topic: Conservation of Mass   Lab: "Reaction in a Bag"

$$C_2H_4O_2 + NaHCO_3 \rightarrow C_2H_3O_2Na + H_2O + CO_2$$

Acetic Acid   Baking Soda   Sodium Acetate   Water   Carbon Dioxide

THE TWO COMPOUNDS ON THE *LEFT* ARE MY REACTANTS...

...AND THESE THREE COMPOUNDS ON THE *RIGHT* ARE MY PRODUCTS.

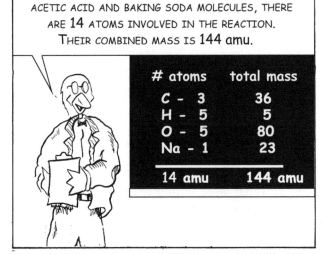

LET'S EXAMINE THE REACTANTS. FOR EVERY PAIR OF ACETIC ACID AND BAKING SODA MOLECULES, THERE ARE 14 ATOMS INVOLVED IN THE REACTION. THEIR COMBINED MASS IS 144 amu.

# atoms	total mass
C - 3	36
H - 5	5
O - 5	80
Na - 1	23
14 amu	144 amu

THE PRODUCTS HAVE THE SAME NUMBER OF ATOMS FOR EACH ELEMENT.

Products:

atoms

144 amu

AND THEREFORE THE SAME MASS.

AND SO WE SEE THAT WITHIN A CLOSED SYSTEM, THE MASS IS CONSERVED IN A CHEMICAL REACTION!

KATZ '05

Dr. Birdley Teaches Science –
Atomic Structure and Chemical Reactions

Objectives

1. To illustrate how molecules change over the course of a reaction.

2. To suggest how one might go about testing the conservation of mass principle.

3. To explain why in a closed system, mass is conserved during a chemical reaction.

4. To introduce concepts of energy changes during a reaction and experimental error.

Synopsis

Dr. Birdley and Anthony conduct an experiment involving a reaction within a plastic bag, in hope of testing the conservation of mass principle.

Main Ideas

1. In a closed system, mass is conserved during a chemical reaction.

2. In a chemical reaction, the same atoms break bonds and form new ones, resulting in new molecules forming.

3. Starting materials are known as reactants, ending materials are known as products.

4. Sometimes improper methods may lead to incorrect results in an experiment.

Vocabulary

products   reactants   conservation of mass

Characters

Dr. Birdley, Anthony, Owelle, Norman

Questions for Discussion

Before Reading:

1. What does it mean to conserve?

2. What happens during a chemical change?

3. What do you think a closed system is? Do they exist in nature?

After Reading:

1. Why did Birdley and Anthony run a reaction in a plastic bag?

2. What sources of error may have been in the experiment?

3. What went wrong with Owelle's experiment?

Dr. Birdley Teaches Science –
Atomic Structure and Chemical Reactions

THE CHEMISTRY EQUATION

Objectives

1. To identify the names and formulas of all the compounds involved in the conservation of mass reaction.

2. To illustrate mathematically why mass is conserved during the reaction.

3. To explain why in a closed system, mass is conserved during a chemical reaction.

4. To demonstrate how the skills of calculating mass and counting atoms can be applied to a chemistry equation.

Synopsis

Dr. Birdley, having been caught by surprise, explains why mass is conserved in the reaction involving hydrochloric acid and baking soda.

Main Ideas

1. In this reaction, acetic acid and baking soda react to form water, carbon dioxide, and sodium acetate.

2. The mass of the products is equal to the mass of the reactants, because the same atoms form the new molecules during the reaction.

3. Mass is conserved during a chemical reaction in a closed system.

Vocabulary

products	reactants	conservation of mass
mass	coefficient	atomic mass units

Characters

Dr. Birdley

Questions for Discussion

Before Reading:

1. What happens during a chemical change?

2. Use a formula and coefficient to represent three molecules of water.

After Reading:

1. How do you know that this process is a chemical change and not a physical change?

2. How does Birdley calculate the mass of the reactants?

3. What is Birdley's main point in illustrating this equation?

Dr. Birdley Teaches Science –
Atomic Structure and Chemical Reactions

Name:_____
Class:_____Date:_____

 **Study Questions**

Directions: Read the related source cartoon and then answer the questions that follow.

  1. What were the two reactants? What happened to them during the comic?

_____

_____

  2. What happens during the chemical reaction?

_____

_____

  3. What did Birdley and Anthony do before and after the reaction? Why?

_____

_____

  4. Why do you think Anthony's bag inflated?

_____

_____

  5. Give one hypothesis as to why Owelle saw such a change in mass during his experiment.

_____

_____

Dr. Birdley Teaches Science –
Atomic Structure and Chemical Reactions

Study Questions

Directions: Read the related source cartoon and then answer the questions that follow.

1. Describe what happens in the chemical equation listed on the board.

_____

_____

2. How many molecules of baking soda react with one molecule of acetic acid? How can you tell?

_____

_____

3. Why would we expect the total mass of the products to be the same as the total mass of the reactants?

_____

_____

4. What are the products in the reaction? Underline the product with the greatest molecular mass.

_____

_____

5. How do you know this chemical reaction is not a physical change?

_____

_____

Dr. Birdley Teaches Science –
Atomic Structure and Chemical Reactions

Background:
Conservation of Mass

During a chemical reaction, **matter is neither created nor destroyed.** Although a new substance is formed, the atoms in the products are the same as those in the reactants. They just recombine to form different molecules. This means that if a reaction is happening in a closed system (such as a sealed bag), the mass of the substances should be the same before and after the reaction.

Dr. Birdley and Anthony demonstrate this principle by finding the mass of the reactants before a chemical reaction, and the mass of the products afterward.

The reactants in this case are **baking soda ($NaHCO_3$)** and **acetic acid ($C_2H_4O_2$),** the active ingredient in vinegar. Anthony "squooshes" the plastic bag in order to mix the two compounds, and they react to form **carbon dioxide (CO_2), water (H_2O),** and **sodium acetate ($C_2H_3O_2Na$).** The bag inflates because the carbon dioxide expands to fill it. The mass stays the same because the "new" products are made of the same atoms as the "old" reactants.

Upon finding the mass of these products, Anthony finds them to be 887.9 g. (The error may have been due to inaccurate measuring or part of the solution escaping. Any other ideas?)

At the end of the comic, Dean Owelle's experiment does not work because his bag was leaking. In this case, the system is no longer closed, and some of his product is not accounted for, resulting in inaccurate data.

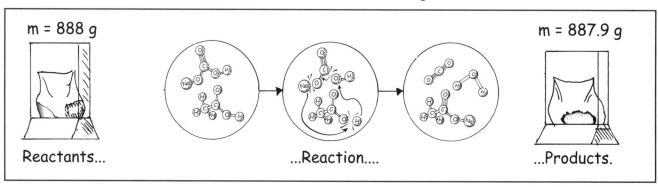

m = 888 g   m = 887.9 g

Reactants...   ...Reaction....   ...Products.

1. What is the central idea of the cartoon?_____

_____

_____

2. What happens to the atoms during the chemical reaction?_____

_____

_____

Name:_____
Class:_____Date:_____

 Vocabulary Build-up!

Directions: Use the following underlined words in sentences that convey their meaning.

1. <u>Reactants</u> are the starting materials that are used to initiate a chemical reaction. Use <u>reactant(s)</u> in a sentence.

_____

_____

2. <u>Products</u> are the new substances that are formed during a chemical reaction. Use <u>products</u> in a sentence.

_____

_____

3. A <u>closed system</u> is a bounded area where no molecules can enter or escape. Give an example of a <u>closed system</u> in a sentence.

_____

_____

4. In a <u>chemical reaction</u>, atoms separate and recombine to form new molecules. Use <u>chemical reaction</u> in a sentence.

_____

_____

5. Mass is <u>conserved</u> in a closed system, meaning that it is neither created nor destroyed. Use <u>conserve</u> or conservation in a <u>sentence</u>.

_____

_____

Dr. Birdley Teaches Science –
Atomic Structure and Chemical Reactions

Practice Problems

Directions: Complete the following exercises to the best of your ability.

3NaHCO₃

Baking Soda

1. The <u>coefficient</u> is a number in front of a formula that indicates how many of those molecules are in the equation. Underline all the coefficients in the space below:

$$H_3C_6H_5O_7 + 3NaHCO_3 \longrightarrow Na_3C_6H_5O_7 + 3H_2O + 3CO_2$$

2. Balance the following equation by adding coefficients so that there are equal numbers of atoms for each element on either side.

__H_2 (hydrogen gas) + __N_2 (nitrogen gas) $\longrightarrow$ __NH_3 (ammonia)

3. Translate the above equation from problem (2) into a sentence.

_____

_____

$H_2O \rightarrow 2H_2 + O_2$

4. Balance the following equation by adding coefficients so that there are equal numbers of atoms for each element on either side.

__Fe (iron) + __O_2 (oxygen gas) $\longrightarrow$ __Fe_2O_3 (rust)

5. Translate the equation in problem four into a sentence.

_____

_____

Dr. Birdley Teaches Science –
Atomic Structure and Chemical Reactions

IN THE SPACE BETWEEN EACH SET OF IMAGES, WRITE A LINKING PHRASE TO CREATE A FACTUAL SENTENCE. USE THE WORD BANK!

PHRASE BANK

ARE BROKEN AND FORMED DURING A

REACTS WITH

TO PRODUCE

IS ALWAYS CONSERVED DURING A

ARE USED TO GENERATE NEW

COMBINE TO FORM

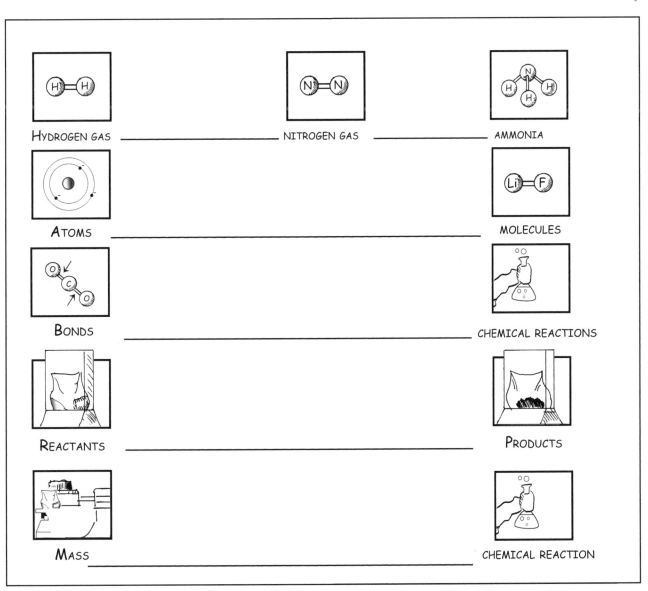

HYDROGEN GAS _____ NITROGEN GAS _____ AMMONIA

ATOMS _____ MOLECULES

BONDS _____ CHEMICAL REACTIONS

REACTANTS _____ PRODUCTS

MASS _____ CHEMICAL REACTION

Dr. Birdley Teaches Science –
Atomic Structure and Chemical Reactions

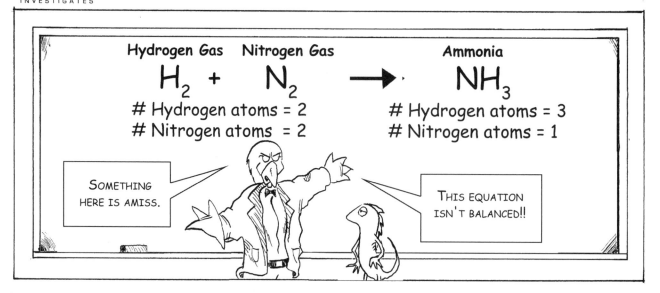

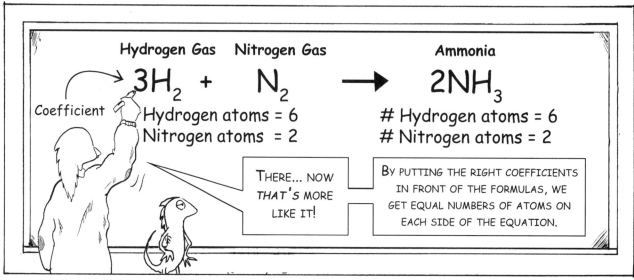

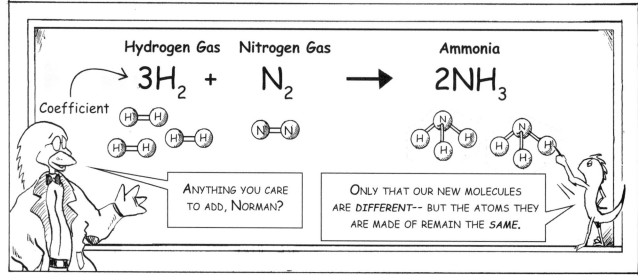

Dr. Birdley Teaches Science –
Atomic Structure and Chemical Reactions

Name:_____

Class:_____Date:_____

Study Questions

Directions: Read the related source cartoon and then answer the questions that follow.

1. Describe what happens in the chemical equation listed on the board.

_____

_____

2a. Why does the equation need to be balanced?

2b. How many molecules of H_2 react with each molecule of N_2?

_____

_____

3. Why would we expect the total mass of the products to be the same as the total mass of the reactants?

_____

_____

4. What changes during this chemical reaction?

_____

_____

5. What central principle mentioned in the comic does a balanced equation illustrate?

_____

_____

Unit 7: Lewis Structures

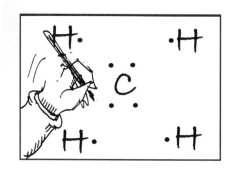

Contents

NAME:_____

CLASS:_____ DATE:_____

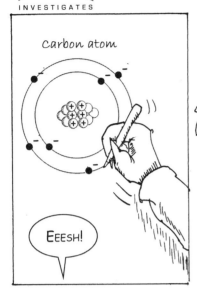

Carbon atom

EEESH!

MY HAND IS GETTING TIRED DRAWING THESE BOHR MODELS! ISN'T THERE AN EASIER WAY TO DRAW ATOMS?

AS A MATTER OF FACT, THERE IS. TRY DRAWING LEWIS STRUCTURES.

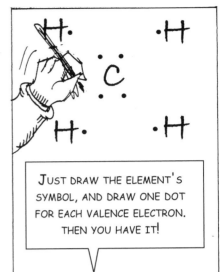

JUST DRAW THE ELEMENT'S SYMBOL, AND DRAW ONE DOT FOR EACH VALENCE ELECTRON. THEN YOU HAVE IT!

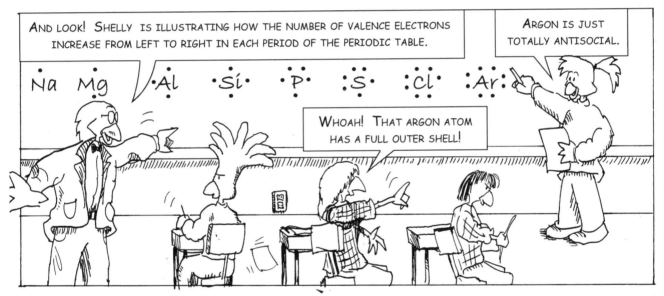

AND LOOK! SHELLY IS ILLUSTRATING HOW THE NUMBER OF VALENCE ELECTRONS INCREASE FROM LEFT TO RIGHT IN EACH PERIOD OF THE PERIODIC TABLE.

ARGON IS JUST TOTALLY ANTISOCIAL.

WHOAH! THAT ARGON ATOM HAS A FULL OUTER SHELL!

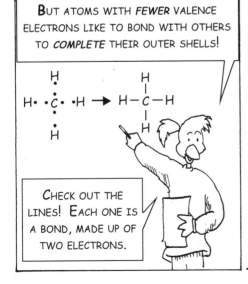

BUT ATOMS WITH *FEWER* VALENCE ELECTRONS LIKE TO BOND WITH OTHERS TO *COMPLETE* THEIR OUTER SHELLS!

CHECK OUT THE LINES! EACH ONE IS A BOND, MADE UP OF TWO ELECTRONS.

WOW. LEWIS STRUCTURES ARE EASIER. MY HAND IS FEELING BETTER ALREADY.

HERE! DONE. 20 MINUTES OF FREE TIME!

WHERE DID I PUT THE CHALLENGE WORK?

Dr. Birdley Teaches Science –
Atomic Structure and Chemical Reactions

Objectives

1. To illustrate how to draw Lewis diagrams of atoms and molecules.

2. To represent the number of valence electrons using the Lewis / electron dot diagram.

3. To use Lewis structures to represent a pattern in the periodic table.

4. To represent molecular bonds using Lewis structures.

Synopsis

Anthony, exhausted from drawing too many Bohr models, learns from Birdley how to draw Lewis structures.

Main Ideas

1. A Lewis structure for a single atom uses the element symbol to represent the atom and dots to represent the valence electrons.

2. Lewis Structures represent the types of atoms and types of bonds in a molecule.

3. In the period from the periodic table (middle panel), the number of valence electrons for a given element increase from left to right.

4. Lewis structures of molecules also show you the number of valence electrons.

5. One single bond represents two valence electrons.

Vocabulary

Lewis structures   valence electrons

Characters

Dr. Birdley, Anthony, Shelly, other students

Questions for Discussion

Before Reading:

1. How long does it take you to draw a Bohr model of carbon?

2. How long does it take you to draw the symbol for carbon and four dots?

After Reading:

1. What pattern shows up on the board in the middle panel?

2. Why does Anthony like Lewis structures?

3. What can Lewis structures tell you that formulas do not?

4. What do Bohr models tell you that Lewis structures do not?

Background: A Structure Named Lewis

Lewis structures can be thought of as a "short-hand" for drawing atoms. Lewis structures help you learn the types of bonds between atoms, and the number of valence electrons in these atoms.

Below is the second major period of the periodic table. Notice how the dots represent only the electrons in the outer energy level, known as **valence electrons.** Look at the contrast between Bohr models and Lewis structures.

Bohr models show you the nucleus and electron energy levels.

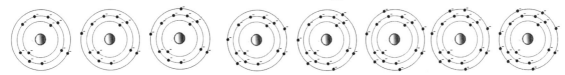

Lewis structures show you the element symbol and the number of valence electrons.

Na   Mg   •Al   •Si•   •P•   :S   :Cl•   :Ar:

Notice the trend: the number of valence electrons increase from left to right. This is important because the number of electrons determine an element's bonding properties.

Lewis structures can also represent molecules. Notice the similarities and differences between the space filling models and Lewis structures below.

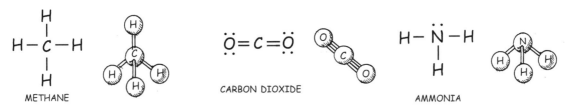

METHANE   CARBON DIOXIDE   AMMONIA

A single bond (-) is made of two electrons and a double bond (=) is made of four valence electrons.

1. Why might Lewis structures be more useful than Bohr models?_____

_____

_____

2. How are Lewis structures different from simply writing the formula?_____

_____

Dr. Birdley Teaches Science –
Atomic Structure and Chemical Reactions

Study Questions

Directions: Read the related source cartoon and then answer the questions that follow.

 1. How is a Lewis structure different from a Bohr model?

_____

_____

 2. Why are Lewis structures useful?

_____

_____

 3. What pattern appears on the board?

_____

_____

 4. Why is argon "antisocial" and "unwilling" to bond with other atoms?

_____

_____

 5. Why does carbon "want" to bond with four other hydrogen atoms?

_____

_____

FOR EACH LEWIS STRUCTURE, GIVE THE FORMULA, THE MOLECULAR MASS, AND THE TOTAL NUMBER OF VALENCE ELECTRONS.

LOOK! A REFERENCE BOX...

Atomic Masses

Carbon - 12   Boron - 11

Oxygen - 16   Flourine - 19

Nitrogen - 14   Hydrogen - 1

A dot ($\cdot$) represents 1 electron

Double bond ($=$) represents 4 electrons

Single bond ($-$) represents 2 electrons

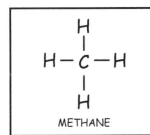

METHANE

O=C=O

CARBON DIOXIDE

H$-$N$-$H

AMMONIA

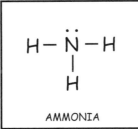

FORMALDEHYDE

1. Formula:_____

Molecular Mass:_____

Valence Electrons:_____

2. Formula:_____

Molecular Mass:_____

Valence Electrons:_____

3. Formula:_____

Molecular Mass:_____

Valence Electrons:_____

4. Formula:_____

Molecular Mass:_____

Valence Electrons:_____

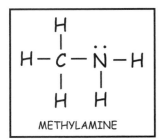

METHYLAMINE

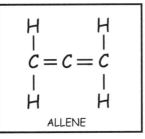

BORON TRIFLUORIDE

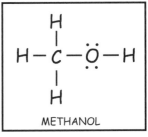

ALLENE

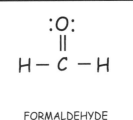

METHANOL

5. Formula:_____

Molecular Mass:_____

Valence Electrons:_____

6. Formula:_____

Molecular Mass:_____

Valence Electrons:_____

7. Formula:_____

Molecular Mass:_____

Valence Electrons:_____

8. Formula:_____

Molecular Mass:_____

Valence Electrons:_____

9. Which molecule has the greatest number of valence electrons?_____

10. Which molecule has the smallest molecular mass?_____

Dr. Birdley Teaches Science –
Atomic Structure and Chemical Reactions

Vocabulary Build-up

Background: A <u>lone pair</u> is a pair of electrons that are not bonded to another atom

A double bond represents two electrons, and a single bond represents four electrons.

Directions: For each molecule, write the number of electrons contained in double bonds, single bonds, and lone pairs.

Molecule	Number of electrons in lone pair	Number of electrons in single bonds	Number of electrons in double bonds
$\ddot{O} = C = \ddot{O}$			
:F: | :F — B — F: 			
:O: || H — C — H			
H $\quad$ H | $\qquad$ | C = C = C | $\qquad$ | H $\quad$ H			
H | H — C — Ö — H | H			

Dr. Birdley Teaches Science –
Atomic Structure and Chemical Reactions

Unit 7 Quiz: Lewis Structures

Directions: Next to each Lewis structure, write the letter of the atom that it represents.

1. ___ Na

2. ___ ·Si·

3. ___ :Cl·

4. ___ :Ar:

a.   b.   c.   d.

For each molecule, write the number of electrons within the double bonds, single bonds, and lone pairs.

Molecule	Number of electrons in lone pair	Number of electrons in single bonds	Number of electrons in double bonds
5. :O: || H – C – H			
6. H | H – C – H | H			
7. H | H – C – Ö – H | H			
8. H | H – C – N̈ – H | | H H			

Answer Key

Answer Key:

Open-ended questions give science students a chance to make connections between new concepts and their personal experiences, as well as to express their answers in different ways. These questions are one important way to differentiate instruction and address different learning styles. However, open-ended questions do not have a single correct answer, so please read student responses carefully to make sure they are not forming misconceptions. One possible correct answer is always given in this answer key

Page 19: Orbitals and Bonding Background Exercise

1. Orbitals are regions of space where electrons are most likely to be found. They are important because how full an orbital is determines how a particular element bonds with other elements.

2. A calcium atom will want to lose its two outer electrons because it would be too difficult to obtain all the electrons needed to fill its outer shell. Instead, it is easier to lose two electrons so the full shell underneath it will serve as the outer shell.

Page 20: The Amazing Atom Study Questions

1. Atoms are important because they are the smallest units of matter.

2. Electrons are different from protons and neutrons because they have a small fraction of their mass and have a negative charge.

3. Electrons stay around the nucleus because of the electrical force the nucleus exerts.

4. An orbital is the region of space around the nucleus where the electrons can usually be found.

5. An atom wants to bond in order to fill its outer electron orbital and achieve a stable octet.

Page 21: Drawing Atoms Visual Exercise – see p. 93

Page 22: The Stable Octet Panel Review

1. The atom identified above is Neon. It has a stable octet because it has a full outer shell, containing eight electrons.

2. The maximum capacity of the inner orbital is two electrons, while the maximum capacity of the outer orbital is eight electrons.

3. The number of electrons each atom would need to gain or lose in order to achieve a stable octet is shown below:

Carbon: gain 4

Nitrogen: gain 3

Oxygen: gain 2

Fluorine: gain 1

Sodium: lose 1

Magnesium: lose 2

Aluminum: lose 3

Page 24: Atomic Structure Quiz

1. d
2. c
3. b
4. c
5. a
6. b

	Mass	Charge	Location
Proton	1 amu	+1	nucleus
Neutron	1 amu	0	nucleus
Electron	1/1836 amu	-1	orbital

Page 30: The Plum Pudding Model Study Questions

1. When Birdley turned on the cathode ray tube, a glowing particle beam appeared that extended from one end of the tube to the other.

2. As the positively charged object was brought closer to the tube, the particle beam bent towards it, revealing that the particles within the beam were negatively charged.

3. Thomson concluded that the beam was made of negative particles that came from within the atom. These particles were originally part of the atom and a great deal smaller than the atom itself.

4. The plum pudding model has tiny negatively charged particles that sit within a diffuse positive charge.

5. The plum pudding model was different from models that came after it because it did not have a nucleus.

Page 31: The Gold Foil Experiment Study Questions

1. Rutherford was conducting the gold foil experiment to learn more about the properties of the atom.

2. In Rutherford's experiment, a particle emitter shot a beam of alpha particles at a piece of gold foil, which was surrounded by a deflection screen.

3. Rutherford obtained evidence by recording the location of flashes on the deflection screen, which indicated the direction of the particles' path after encountering the gold foil.

4. The experiment disproved his hypothesis. Whereas Rutherford thought all the particles would sail through the gold foil, a small number of them bounced off it.

5. Because the particles were deflected by the nucleus, the small proportion of particles that bounced off the gold foil suggest that the nucleus was small compared to the rest of the atom.

Page 32: Early Models and Bonding Background Exercise

1. The Rutherford model is different from the Plum Pudding model because it has a hard positively charged center instead of a more spread out positive charge.

2. Dalton's model is simpler than both Thomson's model and Rutherford's model because it does not have subatomic particles.

Page 33: Atom Experiments & Models Visual Exercise – see p. 93

Page 34: Early Models of the Atom Quiz

1. d
2. b
3. c
4. b
5. b; Dalton's Model
6. a; Plum Pudding model
7. c; Rutherford's model
8. d; deflection screen
9. a; gold foil
10. a; particle emitter
11. b; slit

Page 40: Defending Bohr Study Questions

1. Owelle disapproves of the Bohr model because he finds it inaccurate and unrealistic.

2. The pictures in Owelle's book represent different shapes of orbitals.

3. Whereas the orbitals in the Bohr model are circular paths of electrons, the orbitals in the electron cloud model are regions of space where electrons are most likely to be found.

4. The Bohr model is useful as a teaching tool because it clearly shows the number of electrons in each orbital and can also accurately show how atoms bond using valence electrons.

Dr. Birdley Teaches Science –
Atomic Structure and Chemical Reactions

5. Dr. Birdley's point about models is that they are not fully accurate. This gives credibility to the Bohr model, because it allows certain aspects of it to be unrealistic.

Page 41: Electron Cloud Model Study Questions

1. Dr. Birdley's balloons represent different types of atomic orbitals.

2. In this case, orbitals are regions of space where electrons are most likely to be found.

3. Erwin Schrodinger came up with the electron cloud model in 1926. His central ideas were that electrons did not travel in circular paths, and that their location could only be measured in terms of probability.

4. The Bohr model is different because it illustrates electrons travelling in continuous, circular paths around the nucleus. The movement of the electron that it represents is incorrect.

5. Quantum mechanics is the branch of physics that can be used to describe the motion of an electron. Celia seemed to find this overwhelming, as evidenced by her running away at the sight of quantum mechanics.

Page 42: Bohr vs. Electron Cloud Model Background Exercise

1. The electron cloud model is different from the Bohr model because it does not depict orbitals as circular paths. Instead, orbitals are regions of space where electrons are most likely to be found, and the location of electrons can only be measured in terms of probability.

2. The Bohr model clearly illustrates an atom's number of electrons and energy levels. However, it does not accurately represent what an orbital is, and does not provide a realistic explanation for electron motion.

Page 43: Models of the Atom Visual Exercise – see p. 93
Page 44: Atomic Models Quiz

	Description of Model	New ideas the model introduced
1. Thomson's P. Pudding Model	negative electrons surrounded by a large positive charge	atoms have small negative particles
2. Rutherford's Model	small positively charged nucleus surrounded by electrons	atoms have a nucleus
3. Bohr's Model	nucleus, made of protons and neutrons, surrounded by electrons in specific orbitals	electrons exist within orbitals
4. Schrodinger's E. Cloud Model	nucleus surrounded by regions of space where electrons are most likely to be found.	electrons do not move in circular paths; their motion can only be described by mathematical equations

5. We still teach the Bohr model today because it is a useful method of clearly representing the number of electrons in different orbitals and showing how atoms bond.

6. c (Bohr)

7. b (Rutherford)

8. a (Electron Cloud Model

Page 48: A Periodic Pattern Background Exercise

1. Lithium and Sodium are similar in that they both only have one valence electron, and are highly reactive with non-metals that want to accept electrons.

2. A sodium atom would readily bond with a chlorine atom in order to achieve a stable electron shell.

Page 49: A Periodic Pattern Study Questions

1. Valence electrons are located in the outer orbitals of the atom.

2. Valence electrons allow atoms to bond and enable them to form molecules.

3. Christina points out that for a given row (period) in the periodic table, the number of valence electrons for each element increases from left to right.

4. The number of valence electrons can tell you about the element's chemical properties. In other words, it would tell you the types of substances that the element would react with.

5. You can predict the properties of any element based on its position in the periodic table because its position provides information on its valence electrons, which determine its reactivity.

Page 50: Describe the Pattern Visual Exercise – see p. 93
Page 52: A Periodic Pattern Quiz

1. a
2. c
3. d
4. a

5. The diagram shows two periods from the periodic table. It shows that from left to right, the number of valence electrons for each element increases. This is important because the number of valence electrons determine the bonding ability of an element, and therefore determine how the element reacts with other elements.

Page 58: Atomic Bonding Study Questions

1. Electrons are important because the allow atoms to bond with each other.

2. Covalent bonds involve atoms sharing electrons, whereas ionic bonds involve one atom donating an electron to another atom.

3. In this case, fluorine becomes the negatively charged ion. Accepting the electron causes it to take on a negative charge because it ends up with more electrons than protons.

4. In this case, lithium becomes the positively charged ion. Accepting the electron causes it to take on a positive charge because it ends up with less electrons than protons.

5. Bonding allows one atom to connect with another atom, leading to the formation of molecules.

Page 59: Ionization Study Questions

1. The lithium atom becomes an ion by losing an electron while bonding to a chlorine atom.

2. The lithium atom wanted to lose an electron in order to achieve a stable outer shell.

3. The lithium atom develops a positive charge because it

has three protons and two electrons. The third proton has a positive charge that is not cancelled by an electron.

4. Lithium ions are more stable than neutral atoms because they have a full outer electron shell.

5. There are fewer neutral lithium atoms around because they are unstable. They usually want to lose an electron and become ions.

Page 60: Background: Ionic and Covalent Bonding

1. Whereas an ionic bond involves an atom giving one or more electrons to another atom, an covalent bond involves two atoms sharing electrons.

2. Lithium takes on a positive charge because it has just lost an electron, and now has more protons than electrons. Fluorine just gained an electron, and takes on a negative charge.

Page 61: Vocabulary & Practice Problems

4: Identify each molecule as ionic or covalent.

a. covalent

b. ionic

c. ionic

d. covalent

e. ionic

f. ionic

g. covalent

h. ionic

5. If calcium loses two electrons, its charge is +2. If chlorine gains one electron, its charge is -1.

Page 62: Ionic Formulas Mini-Comic

1. An ion is different from a normal atom because it has a positive or negative charge because it has lost or gained electrons.

2. You know you've written an ionic formula correctly when the positive charge balances (or cancels out) the negative charge.

3. $CaCl_2$

4. Li_2O

Page 63: Becoming an Ion Visual Exercise – see p. 94

Page 64: Practice with Ionic Formulas Visual Exercise – see p. 94

Page 65: Panel Review: Ions

1. Lithium, Fluorine, Hydrogen, Oxygen, Hydrogen

2. Lithium

3. Fluorine

4. Ionic

5. One atom has a positive charge because it lost an electron, and has one less electron than it does protons.

6. One atom has a negative charge because it gained an electron, and has one more electron than it does protons.

7. Atoms want to bond to achieve full and stable electron shells.

Page 66: Bonding Quiz

1. a

2. c

3. b

4. b

5. d

6. a

7. ionic

8. covalent

Page 72: Conservation of Mass Study Questions

1. The two reactants were acetic acid and baking soda. In the reaction, they were used to make carbon dioxide, water, and sodium acetate.

2. During the chemical reaction, several of the bonds connecting

the atoms break apart. The atoms create new bonds at different locations, forming new molecules.

3. Birdley and Anthony found the mass of the substances before and after the reaction to see if it would change during the process.

4. The bag inflated because of the carbon dioxide gas released during the reaction.

5. Owelle saw a change in mass because he had a hole in his bag. Some of the substances leaked out, resulting in inaccurate data.

Page 73: The Chemical Equation Study Questions

1. In the chemical equation listed on the board, acetic acid and baking soda are used to produce carbon dioxide, water, and sodium acetate.

2. One molecule of baking soda reacts with one molecule of acetic acid. You can tell because there are no coefficients in front of the formulas.

3. The total mass of the products would be the same as those of the reactants because mass is neither created nor destroyed during the reaction.

4. The products in the reaction are water, carbon dioxide, and sodium acetate.

Page 74: Conservation of Mass Background Exercise

1. The central idea of the cartoon is that the mass is neither created nor destroyed during a chemical reaction, and that the mass of the products should be equal to the mass of the starting materials if there is no error in the procedure.

2 During a chemical reaction, some atoms will break up and recombine to form new molecules.

Page 76: The Chemical Equation Practice Problems

1. $\underline{1}H_3C_6O_7$, $\underline{3}NaHCO_3$, $\underline{1}Na_3C_6H_5O_7$, $\underline{3}H_2O$, $\underline{3}CO_2$

2. $\underline{3}H_2$, $\underline{1}N_2$, $\underline{2}NH_3$

3. Nitrogen gas reacts with hydrogen gas to produce ammonia.

4. $\underline{4}Fe$, $\underline{3}O_2$, $\underline{2}Fe_2O_3$

5. Iron reacts with oxygen gas to produce rust.

Page 79: The Balancing Act Study Questions

1. In the chemical reaction on the board, a diatomic nitrogen molecule (N_2) combines with three diatomic hydrogen molecules to form two ammonia molecules (NH_3).

2a. The equation needs to be balanced so that there are equal numbers of atoms for each element on either side.

2b. Three molecules of H_2 will react with every molecule of N_2.

3. We should expect the total mass of products to be the same as the total mass of reactants because both products and reactants have the same number of atoms for each element.

4. In this chemical reaction, the H_2 and N_2 molecules break down, and atoms they were made of recombine to form two molecules of NH_3.

5. A balanced equation illustrates that in the mass and the number of atoms is always conserved in a chemical reaction. In other words, mass is neither created nor destroyed.

Page 83: A Structure Name Lewis Background Exercise

1. Lewis Structures might be more useful than Bohr models because they are easier to illustrate, they represent electrons more clearly, and they can be easily used to represent molecules as well.

2. Lewis Structures are different from writing the chemical formula because instead of just representing the number of atoms in a molecule, they illustrate the molecule's basic structure.

Answer Key

Page 84: A Structure Named Lewis Study Questions

1. While a Bohr model represents the nucleus and the electron orbitals, the Lewis structure uses a symbol for the element and dots for electrons.

2. Lewis structures are useful because they are an efficient way of representing the atoms and their valence electrons. They can also be used to represent the structures of simple molecules.

3. The pattern on the board shows that going across a period from left to right, the number of valence electrons for a given element increases.

4. Argon is "antisocial" because it has a full outer shell (stable octet) and does not want to bond with other atoms.

5. Carbon wants to bond with four other valence electrons so that it can achieve a full outer shell (stable octet).

Page 85: Analyzing Lewis Structures Visual Exercise – see p. 94

Page 86: Vocabulary Build-up

Background: A <u>lone pair</u> is a pair of electrons that are not bonded to another atom

A double bond represents two electrons, and a single bond represents four electrons.

Directions: For each molecule, write the number of electrons contained in double bonds, single bonds, and lone pairs.

Molecule	Number of electrons in lone pair	Number of electrons in single bonds	Number of electrons in double bonds
$\ddot{O}=C=\ddot{O}$	8	0	8
:F: | :F–B–F:	18	6	0
:O: || H–C–H	4	4	4
H H | | C=C=C | | H H	0	8	8
H | H–C–O–H | H	4	10	0

Page 87: Lewis Structures Quiz

1. b
2. d
3. a
4. c
5. 4, 4, 4
6. 0, 8, 0
7. 4, 10, 0
8. 2, 12, 0

Page 21 Drawing Atoms

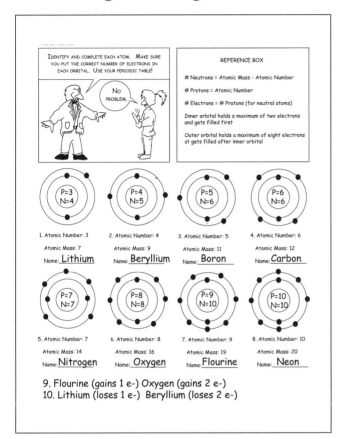

IDENTIFY AND COMPLETE EACH ATOM. MAKE SURE YOU PUT THE CORRECT NUMBER OF ELECTRONS IN EACH ORBITAL. USE YOUR PERIODIC TABLE!

No PROBLEM.

REFERENCE BOX

Neutrons = Atomic Mass - Atomic Number

Protons = Atomic Number

Electrons = # Protons (for neutral atoms)

Inner orbital holds a maximum of two electrons and gets filled first

Outer orbital holds a maximum of eight electrons at gets filled after inner orbital

P=3 N=4 — 1. Atomic Number: 3, Atomic Mass: 7, Name: Lithium

P=4 N=5 — 2. Atomic Number: 4, Atomic Mass: 9, Name: Beryllium

P=5 N=6 — 3. Atomic Number: 5, Atomic Mass: 11, Name: Boron

P=6 N=6 — 4. Atomic Number: 6, Atomic Mass: 12, Name: Carbon

P=7 N=7 — 5. Atomic Number: 7, Atomic Mass: 14, Name: Nitrogen

P=8 N=8 — 6. Atomic Number: 8, Atomic Mass: 16, Name: Oxygen

P=9 N=10 — 7. Atomic Number: 9, Atomic Mass: 19, Name: Flourine

P=10 N=10 — 8. Atomic Number: 10, Atomic Mass: 20, Name: Neon

9. Flourine (gains 1 e-) Oxygen (gains 2 e-)
10. Lithium (loses 1 e-) Beryllium (loses 2 e-)

Page 33 Atom Experiments and Models

THESE TWO EXPERIMENTS RESULTED IN NEW ATOMIC MODELS. LABEL EACH SETUP AND MODEL WITH THE CORRECT PARTS! USE THE WORD BANK.

WORD BANK

GOLD FOIL	SLIT
PLUM PUDDING MODEL	RUTHERFORD'S MODEL
DEFLECTION SCREEN	ELECTRON (2)
CATHODE RAY TUBE	POSITIVE NUCLEUS
POSITIVE OBJECT	POSITIVE CLOUD
PARTICLE BEAM	ALPHA PARTICLE EMITTER

1. CATHODE RAY TUBE   2. POSITIVE OBJECT
3. PARTICLE BEAM

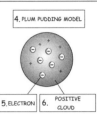

4. PLUM PUDDING MODEL
5. ELECTRON   6. POSITIVE CLOUD

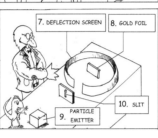

7. DEFLECTION SCREEN   8. GOLD FOIL
9. PARTICLE EMITTER   10. SLIT

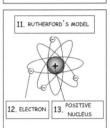

11. RUTHERFORD'S MODEL
12. ELECTRON   13. POSITIVE NUCLEUS

Page 43 Models of the Atom

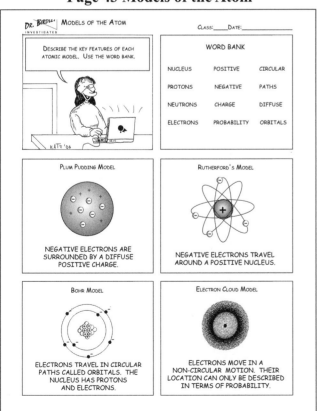

DR. BIRDLEY INVESTIGATES   MODELS OF THE ATOM   CLASS:_____ DATE:_____

DESCRIBE THE KEY FEATURES OF EACH ATOMIC MODEL. USE THE WORD BANK.

WORD BANK

NUCLEUS	POSITIVE	CIRCULAR
PROTONS	NEGATIVE	PATHS
NEUTRONS	CHARGE	DIFFUSE
ELECTRONS	PROBABILITY	ORBITALS

PLUM PUDDING MODEL

NEGATIVE ELECTRONS ARE SURROUNDED BY A DIFFUSE POSITIVE CHARGE.

RUTHERFORD'S MODEL

NEGATIVE ELECTRONS TRAVEL AROUND A POSITIVE NUCLEUS.

BOHR MODEL

ELECTRONS TRAVEL IN CIRCULAR PATHS CALLED ORBITALS. THE NUCLEUS HAS PROTONS AND ELECTRONS.

ELECTRON CLOUD MODEL

ELECTRONS MOVE IN A NON-CIRCULAR MOTION. THEIR LOCATION CAN ONLY BE DESCRIBED IN TERMS OF PROBABILITY.

Page 50 Describe the Pattern

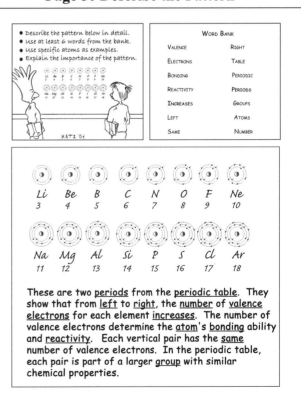

- Describe the pattern below in detail.
- Use at least 6 words from the bank.
- Use specific atoms as examples.
- Explain the importance of the pattern.

WORD BANK

VALENCE	RIGHT
ELECTRONS	TABLE
BONDING	PERIODIC
REACTIVITY	PERIODS
INCREASES	GROUPS
LEFT	ATOMS
SAME	NUMBER

Li 3   Be 4   B 5   C 6   N 7   O 8   F 9   Ne 10

Na 11   Mg 12   Al 13   Si 14   P 15   S 16   Cl 17   Ar 18

These are two <u>periods</u> from the <u>periodic table</u>. They show that from <u>left</u> to <u>right</u>, the <u>number</u> of <u>valence electrons</u> for each element <u>increases</u>. The number of valence electrons determine the <u>atom's</u> <u>bonding</u> ability and <u>reactivity</u>. Each vertical pair has the <u>same</u> number of valence electrons. In the periodic table, each pair is part of a larger <u>group</u> with similar chemical properties.

Dr. Birdley Teaches Science –
Atomic Structure and Chemical Reactions

Page 63 Becoming an Ion

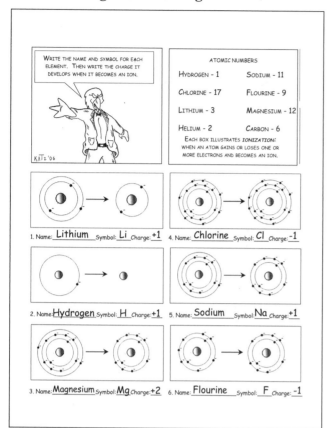

WRITE THE NAME AND SYMBOL FOR EACH ELEMENT. THEN WRITE THE CHARGE IT DEVELOPS WHEN IT BECOMES AN ION.

ATOMIC NUMBERS

HYDROGEN - 1   SODIUM - 11

CHLORINE - 17   FLOURINE - 9

LITHIUM - 3   MAGNESIUM - 12

HELIUM - 2   CARBON - 6

EACH BOX ILLUSTRATES *IONIZATION:* WHEN AN ATOM GAINS OR LOSES ONE OR MORE ELECTRONS AND BECOMES AN ION.

1. Name: Lithium Symbol: Li Charge: +1

2. Name: Hydrogen Symbol: H Charge: +1

3. Name: Magnesium Symbol: Mg Charge: +2

4. Name: Chlorine Symbol: Cl Charge: -1

5. Name: Sodium Symbol: Na Charge: +1

6. Name: Flourine Symbol: F Charge: -1

Page 64 Practice with Ionic Formulas

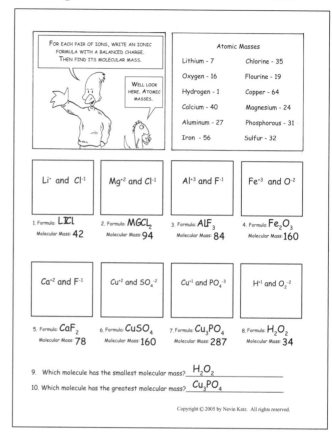

FOR EACH PAIR OF IONS, WRITE AN IONIC FORMULA WITH A BALANCED CHARGE. THEN FIND ITS MOLECULAR MASS.

WELL LOOK HERE. ATOMIC MASSES.

Atomic Masses

Lithium - 7   Chlorine - 35

Oxygen - 16   Flourine - 19

Hydrogen - 1   Copper - 64

Calcium - 40   Magnesium - 24

Aluminum - 27   Phosphorous - 31

Iron - 56   Sulfur - 32

Li^+ and Cl^{-1} — 1. Formula: $LiCl$ Molecular Mass: 42

Mg^{+2} and Cl^{-1} — 2. Formula: $MgCl_2$ Molecular Mass: 94

Al^{+3} and F^{-1} — 3. Formula: AlF_3 Molecular Mass: 84

Fe^{+3} and O^{-2} — 4. Formula: Fe_2O_3 Molecular Mass: 160

Ca^{+2} and F^{-1} — 5. Formula: CaF_2 Molecular Mass: 78

Cu^{+2} and SO_4^{-2} — 6. Formula: $CuSO_4$ Molecular Mass: 160

Cu^{+1} and PO_4^{-3} — 7. Formula: Cu_3PO_4 Molecular Mass: 287

H^{+1} and O_2^{-2} — 8. Formula: H_2O_2 Molecular Mass: 34

9. Which molecule has the smallest molecular mass? H_2O_2

10. Which molecule has the greatest molecular mass? Cu_3PO_4

Page 77 Chemical Reactions: Linking Images

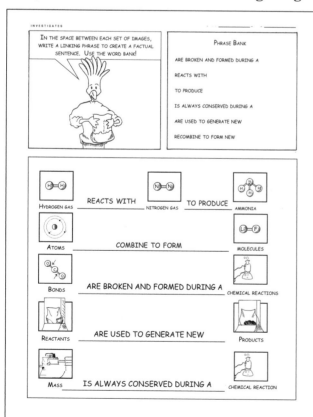

INVESTIGATE!

IN THE SPACE BETWEEN EACH SET OF IMAGES, WRITE A LINKING PHRASE TO CREATE A FACTUAL SENTENCE. USE THE WORD BANK!

PHRASE BANK

ARE BROKEN AND FORMED DURING A

REACTS WITH

TO PRODUCE

IS ALWAYS CONSERVED DURING A

ARE USED TO GENERATE NEW

RECOMBINE TO FORM NEW

HYDROGEN GAS — REACTS WITH — NITROGEN GAS — TO PRODUCE — AMMONIA

ATOMS — COMBINE TO FORM — MOLECULES

BONDS — ARE BROKEN AND FORMED DURING A — CHEMICAL REACTIONS

REACTANTS — ARE USED TO GENERATE NEW — PRODUCTS

MASS — IS ALWAYS CONSERVED DURING A — CHEMICAL REACTION

Page 85 Analyzing Lewis Structures

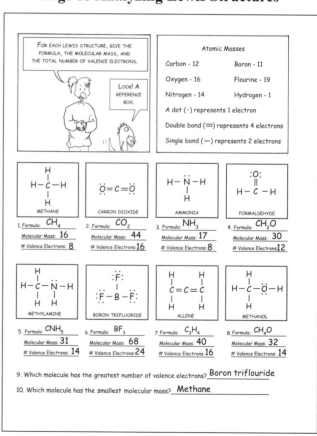

FOR EACH LEWIS STRUCTURE, GIVE THE FORMULA, THE MOLECULAR MASS, AND THE TOTAL NUMBER OF VALENCE ELECTRONS.

LOOK! A REFERENCE BOX.

Atomic Masses

Carbon - 12   Boron - 11

Oxygen - 16   Flourine - 19

Nitrogen - 14   Hydrogen - 1

A dot (·) represents 1 electron

Double bond ($=$) represents 4 electrons

Single bond ($-$) represents 2 electrons

METHANE — 1. Formula: CH_4 — Molecular Mass: 16 — # Valence Electrons: 8

CARBON DIOXIDE — 2. Formula: CO_2 — Molecular Mass: 44 — # Valence Electrons: 16

AMMONIA — 3. Formula: NH_3 — Molecular Mass: 17 — # Valence Electrons: 8

FORMALDEHYDE — 4. Formula: CH_2O — Molecular Mass: 30 — # Valence Electrons: 12

METHYLAMINE — 5. Formula: CNH_5 — Molecular Mass: 31 — # Valence Electrons: 14

BORON TRIFLUORIDE — 6. Formula: BF_3 — Molecular Mass: 68 — # Valence Electrons: 24

ALLENE — 7. Formula: C_3H_4 — Molecular Mass: 40 — # Valence Electrons: 16

METHANOL — 8. Formula: CH_4O — Molecular Mass: 32 — # Valence Electrons: 14

9. Which molecule has the greatest number of valence electrons? Boron triflouride

10. Which molecule has the smallest molecular mass? Methane

Dr. Birdley Teaches Science –
Atomic Structure and Chemical Reactions